Christof Wolf, S.J.
The Moment Is For Me

Christof Wolf, S.J.

The Moment Is For Me

Imprimatur. Paderbornae, d. 29. m. Ianuarii 2014
Nr. A 58-21.00.2/913. Vicarius Generalis Alfons Hardt

Illustrations: Monika Gatt
Title design: Monika Gatt and Christof Wolf, S.J.

Translation: Daniel Jamros, S.J.

ISBN 978-3-939926-12-2

For Adelheid and Berthold

Self-realization is the ultimate fact of facts. An actuality is self-realizing, and whatever is self-realizing is an actuality.

Alfred North Whitehead, Process and Reality

If God finds man ready,
he does not look at
what he was before.
God is a God of the present.
As he finds you
he takes you and receives you,
not as who you were,
but as who you are now.

German mysticism

TABLE OF CONTENTS

INTRODUCTION

Much has been written about "The Power and Secret of the Jesuits." But perhaps not everything is secret, because what constitutes the Jesuits above all is their common spiritual foundation, the Exercises of Saint Ignatius (1491-1556), who founded the Jesuit order.

Every Jesuit makes the so-called "Full Spiritual Exercises" twice in his life, at the beginning and end of his formation. He spends thirty days in silence and prayer, centered on his relation to God and Jesus. He ponders the decisive question: what is God's will for me and my life? Am I called to be a Jesuit, a companion of Jesus?

Silence is more than mere not-speaking: it opens a man to a new dimension in his life. Extended silence enables one to hear. Forty days before his public appearance, Jesus himself was led into stillness and solitude in the desert. His desert experience with the three temptations is certainly a key event in his life. All three temptations concern the first commandment: "I am the LORD your God. You shall not have other gods beside me! You shall not make for yourself an idol to worship." For Jesus God alone counts, not the apotheosis of earthly power and whatever accompanies it. A human who can turn stone into bread can also rule the world with "bread and circuses." Jesus had the ability to do so, but he refused to use it, even for his own hunger. True bread, true security, comes from God alone. Knowing this, Jesus proclaims: "This is the time of fulfillment. The kingdom of God is at hand. Repent, and believe in the good news." People who heed this call and re-orient themselves accordingly feel an inner freedom, liberated from every dependence and compulsion.

In the Spiritual Exercises, we share this basic experience of Jesus in the desert. The gift of inner freedom expresses itself as gratitude, kindness, patience, perseverance, generosity, and affability. That inner freedom is the foundation for seeking and finding God in all things. It enables us to work "Ad majorem Dei gloriam" ("For the greater glory of God") with "indifference," which means not that everything is of no interest to me, but that everything is of equal interest for me. I meet everything with the same openness. If I lose my soul to something other than God, in the end I lose my inner freedom.

For Ignatius the key to keeping that freedom is the virtue of humility. He distinguishes three kinds of humility. The first is to live so that I keep all of God's commandments, even if I were offered power over the whole world. I resist temptation as Jesus did, when Satan offered him all the kingdoms of the world if he would only worship him instead of God. The second kind of humility is complete indifference: wealth or poverty, health or sickness, a short or long life — I do not strive for one more than for another. Fanaticism and fundamentalism have no place here, because they lack this indifference. The third kind includes the first and second: I always try to become more like Jesus, even when the world considers me foolish or crazy for doing so. At no time was the following of Jesus easy. Many turned away from him, even in his lifetime, because following Jesus means a radical orientation for God.

The community that Ignatius founded with his companions has more than spiritual exercises for its foundation. Along with the vows of poverty and celibacy, obedience above all is central for every Jesuit. The key is again the model of Jesus, who learned obedience by facing the cross: "not my will, but your will be done," says Jesus. Many interpret this passage as the greatest abandonment by God that Jesus experienced in his life. But God was never closer to him as in Gethsemane. Only in his decision was Jesus alone. His Father could not make it for him, just because he had to take the suffering upon himself. Jesus could have run away from it, but he accepted his Father's will.

RELIGIOUS EXPERIENCE

The question of a radical following of Jesus is central for a novice who thinks about entering the Jesuit order. Nevertheless, the Exercises are not only for Jesuits, but are also offered to anyone seeking religious experience. In general, they help us reorient our lives to God. They are no abstract theory, but are grounded in Ignatius's life experience. In 1521, he was wounded by a cannonball while serving as a soldier in a battle in Pamplona. During his convalescence, he read about the life of Jesus and the lives of saints. After his recovery, he began to lead a strict ascetical life, wanting to imitate Saint Francis and Saint Dominic. He then had an experience that marked and changed his entire life. He later wrote about this experience in the third person:

> *This event was so powerful … it was as though he became a different man and acquired an understanding entirely different from what he had possessed earlier. Illuminated by God, he began to view the things of God with entirely different eyes — learning to discover the good and the evil spirits. Tasting the things of God within, he wanted to impart them to his fellow humans.*

He now realized that we can find God in all things. His experiences led to an "instruction" for prayer, the "Spiritual Exercises." They assume that God is immediately accessible to his creatures — not only to a saint, but to everyone. Also new was the type and method of religious experience that they promote: Ignatius calls it "praying with all our senses." He thus developed further the method of meditative prayer known since the Desert Fathers as the "Lectio Divina." This method consisted of four steps: *lectio* (reading), *meditatio* (meditation), *oratio* (prayer), and *contemplatio* (contemplation). After an attentive reading of a Bible passage, we select a verse that especially speaks to us and meditate on it, by reflecting on it repeatedly. For Ignatius, the reflective meditation makes use of all the senses in prayer: seeing, hearing, smelling, tasting, and touching. Reflecting on the word of God leads to the prayer, and in the stillness of the contemplation the person praying experiences communion with God.

IGNATIAN WAYS OF PRAYER

In the Exercises, the exercitant is invited to pray for an hour four times during the day. Ignatius developed a precise method for prayer, illustrated by the following texts in italics from his book of Exercises. For contemporary readers, they may sound harsh, but they give us a good impression of his style.

It [the exercise] comprises a preparatory prayer and two preludes, three main points, and a colloquy.

THE PREPARATORY PRAYER IS: to ask God our Lord for the grace that all my intentions, actions, and activities be purely directed to the service and praise of his divine majesty.

THE FIRST PRELUDE IS: composition of place, by imagining the scene. Here note: … when one considers Christ our Lord … the composition will consist in seeing the physical place with the eye of imagination … for example, a temple or mountain where Jesus is.

THE SECOND PRELUDE IS: to ask God our Lord for what I want and wish. The request must correspond to the underlying material of the meditation.

This means: when the meditation concerns the resurrection, to ask God for joy with Christ joyful; when it concerns the Passion, to ask for anguish, tears, and torment with the tormented Christ.

THE MAIN POINTS ARE: to see, observe, and consider what the persons

Let us review the structure we have just described. After selecting a Bible passage, one begins with the preparatory prayer, asking for an appropriate inner orientation to God. Making up one's own preparatory prayer can be a small initial spiritual exercise. The prayer doesn't always have to be completely new, as long as it continues one's path of prayer. In this dynamic, our own limitations might get a new perspective: something new and unexpected can be given to me. I should also ask for that and be ready for it.

I then compose the scene, furnished like a stage or a film set. I imagine a concrete place corresponding to the content of the selected Bible passage. Each place has its own atmosphere: it feels wide or narrow, comfortable or threatening, warm or cold, and has its own distinctive odor.

Using this method, it is easy to get lost in one's fantasy, since Ignatius brings us actively into the scene. I should not ask for just anything, but for the gift of feeling the scene. Real empathy with it involves my emotions and has the potential to change me and give me new perspectives.

Once the stage setting or film location is ready, I consider who is there to see. What are the actors saying? What especially speaks to me?

After the words comes the action. Now begins the inner film, the main part of the exercise. Like a director or cameraman, I shape my own film. I let myself speak with the persons, interact with them, grasp them, touch them, or just let myself observe them. Ignatius's recommendation to "reflect on myself" means that I let my emotions really encounter the story, which can make me laugh or cry. And in spite of precise planning, surprises keep coming up, just as in a real filming where the story might get a completely new ending.

Every prayer exercise closes with a short colloquy. One reviews the just-completed prayer and puts into words what the heart says, as though one were speaking to a good friend. As Ignatius recommends, one can speak to the Father, Son, Holy Spirit, Mary, or even to a person who was on the stage or film set of your imagination. It's almost like what Heinrich von Kleist writes in his essay "On the Gradual Production of Thoughts While Speaking": "there is a strange source of inspiration for a speaker in the human face of the listener: a glance telling us that a half-expressed thought has already been understood often provides us the expression for the other half." One does not yet know exactly what to communicate, but the benevolent listener helps me formulate insights, desires, and requests that I would never come upon on my own. That's exactly what happens in conversation.

The conclusion is an "Our Father" — perhaps the oldest prayer of the church, taught by Jesus to his disciples. Praying from the heart also means praying with the words of Jesus.

After the time of prayer, Ignatius recommends a short period of reflection, lasting about fifteen minutes. I review and reflect on what has happened, on what has been given me. What were the good experiences in the prayer? The irritating ones? It is helpful to keep a spiritual diary, lest nuances get forgotten. With a diary I can more easily recognize my life themes, and even discover a central thread.

A vivid analogy to the structure of Ignatian prayer is the invitation to a party. The preparatory prayer is my thinking about what to wear, an outfit that suits the occasion and the host. After my arrival I first look around the place and orient myself. Now I have to decide what to do first: go to the bar and order a drink, or greet friends, etc. Then the party begins for me. I listen, converse, and laugh, until the party ends. On the way home I speak with my best friend about the party. Together we consider what we experienced, what especially touched us, what went especially well. At home I write down the most important experiences in my diary.

EVERYTHING WITHOUT PRESSURE

Ignatius's instructions may seem somewhat complicated; they do demand some time for practice. Not for nothing are they called spiritual *exercises*. But an exercitant is also freed from the pressure that every effort must immediately be crowned with success. In the Exercises there are times of consolation, and times of dryness. Ever optimistic, Ignatius advises me in times of dryness to remember the times of consolation. People who see only the negative side of things will hardly ever experience a change for the better. A good thing needs exercise, time, and patience: that is an old piece of folk wisdom, and also typically Ignatian. The "Full Exercises" are a classic example.

No matter how dense the exercise, one does not have to accomplish anything in it. I can stop my interior film anytime, and take a rest — especially when I feel deep joy, beauty, harmony, consolation, sympathy, and love. In these moments, my soul is touched by God. For Ignatius, it comes down to intensity and fulfillment: it is not much knowledge that satisfies the soul, but feeling and tasting the things within, he says. Thus it is consistent for Ignatius to recommend the repetition of each exercise, which often becomes more simple and more intense the second time around. It's like seeing a film for the second time: I get a broader view and notice many things that eluded me the first time.

A religious experience using all our senses opens the door to the deeper levels of our life. We are especially helped by imagining a scene where God is met. As Moses stood amazed before the burning bush, so can our imagination create places in which we encounter God. Consequently the first suggestion is always the invitation to create our own scene. I can concretely imagine a desert, in order to encounter Jesus there. First I ask myself: how does the desert look? Is it a sandy desert, a thorny cactus desert, or more of a steppe? Is the sun shining? Is there a shady spot? Is it unbearably hot? My sensitivity can see and feel the subtleties of a scene, and touch it with my own emotions.

Can I see Jesus? Perhaps he is only a small black dot on the horizon and I must open myself to seeking him. Do I even want to go into the desert with him, or do I feel inner resistance? Perhaps I also find myself sitting next to Jesus in the desert. I can lean on him, touch him, or let him touch me. I can begin a conversation with him, or perhaps ask Jesus what I always wanted to ask him. I can laugh and cry with Jesus or just be with him. Or perhaps walk together with him a bit, looking for water.

Before I dive into an exercise, I ask for the readiness to grow in my capacity for love, my capacity for sympathy. Opening myself up always makes me vulnerable and pliable.

In this way prayer is a creative, dynamic, and open process. "My entire life is a receipt without my signature," writes the Portuguese author Fernando Pessoa. Prayer stretches one out towards a future that one would like to realize, and this can be experienced only by doing the exercise. In this way of prayer the person praying receives something that is accessible only to himself and God, and that cannot be predicted.

"THE FULL EXERCISES" IN DAILY LIFE

Ignatius divides the "Full Exercises" into four weeks, and gives them a thematic structure. The first week considers the Principle and Foundation; the second week, the life of Jesus; the third week, his Passion; the fourth week, his resurrection. The first week concerns me and my relation to God. In the second week, I try to find traces of my own life in the concrete life of Jesus. The third week invites me to accompany Jesus in the pain and suffering of his last hours, up to the cross. The fourth week, to share in the transformation from death to life, to experience joy and love in the new life of the resurrection. Moreover, the thirty days do not have to be divided into four equal periods of time; in practice, one or another week can take longer than seven days. The other weeks then become correspondingly shorter.

Ignatius's book of Exercises is freely available, but the Spiritual Exercises can hardly be made alone; they need instruction and accompaniment. Nevertheless, anyone can integrate the inner creative process of the Exercises into daily spiritual life. The themes presented here are a "translation" of the "Full Exercises" for daily life, and can accompany and inspire anyone who wants to follow them.

In the following Exercises, each day in the individual weeks has a theme, which normally begins with a Bible text. A brief suggestion and concrete questions invite one deeper. They are somewhat unfinished, aiming only to be part of a process.

Of course the basic theme of each week is present in all the subordinate daily themes. One acquires a taste for the weekly theme only after sampling it in the daily themes. It is also not necessary to go through the Exercises in four calendar weeks. In daily life they may be extended into a longer time frame.

One should also be flexible about performing the daily Exercises. Resolving to do them on a regular basis can produce a guilty conscience if I soon become unfaithful to my resolutions — as will surely happen if my zeal has taken too much upon itself, and overloaded my agenda. For the Exercises in daily life one thing counts above all: what I undertake must be feasible for me. Less is often more in the spiritual life; a brief intense conversation with God can be more helpful than a prayer time completed according to plan.

Here too is the decision for a concrete place of prayer important. Where can I find a quiet break for a few minutes of silence away from the day's business? How much of the prayer can I bring back into my day? This all has to be tried out before settling on an appropriate routine.

One can probably schedule a longer prayer time in the morning, before work begins, and again in the evening, to review the day. Then the Bible text or a question from the morning meditation will stay with me during the day, now and then coming to the surface. Perhaps they will take on a new light in situations related to them. Ignatian spirituality sharpens our eye for what is essential in daily life. It teaches us to be alert in the here and now, so that we can say with Andreas Gryphius: "the moment is for me. I use it carefully, so it belongs to me: in time and in eternity."

An introduction to a sensory experience of God can use more than language. The aquarelles by the artist Monika Gatt are therefore provided as an invitation to pictorial contemplation. Since they depict only excerpts from a larger whole, they loosen the imagination. They encourage us to grapple with an unfinished work, and to be creative with ourselves.

I have often referred to theater and film in order to describe praying with the senses. Although viewing a film is not prayer — my senses get overpowered by the director's vision — I can let myself be touched by the characters and their stories, and often identify myself with them. I can also use my experience of them in prayer, as I do with a Bible passage. In the so-called "Film-Exercises," films provide motifs for prayer. In this book, films are mentioned at the end of the daily meditations, to provide help and further stimulation to exercitants who love cinema.

FIRST WEEK:
PRINCIPLE AND FOUNDATION

Ignatius writes at the beginning of the first week of the Exercises: "Man is created to praise God." We are creatures of God, images of God and created for God. God is our foundation, for our dignity comes to us only from God. No one else can give it to us, no one can take it from us. God invites us to become like him: to love, to do good, to be creative, to shape creation, to meet every situation with a loving gaze. We try to see the world with "God's eyes." Then, aware of goodness, I become grateful: I do not owe my life to myself, but to the loving devotion of two people; and ultimately to God.

For Ignatius gratitude is always the starting point of prayer. A discontented person circles only around himself, and wants no change. He makes the world into something like himself — not that the world is really like that, but because his pessimism allows nothing to change.

Often discontent goes hand in hand with envy. Those who are envious only see the greener grass on the other side. But the fact that I want to have what someone else has indicates that the goal I am striving for is not mine and does not suit me and my life. Envy prevents my own creative process from beginning. It keeps me lost in other people's goals and prevents me from seeing what I am actually called to do. Envious people are not creative.

In the first week I also face my dark sides. This requires courage and strength and above all honesty. Ignatius invites us to look realistically at ourselves, at what we fail to do, even when we know better in our heart. At the end of the first week Ignatius therefore suggests making a general confession, something hard for us to imagine today. However, a radical new beginning requires reconciliation with myself, my fellow men, and with God. The door is open, but the individual has to go through it, in order to take the path towards new inner freedom.

MEDITATION 1

Psalm 139

LORD, you have probed me, you know me:
> 2 you know when I sit and stand;
> you understand my thoughts from afar.
3 You sift through my travels and my rest;
> with all my ways you are familiar.
4 Even before a word is on my tongue,
> LORD, you know it all.
5 Behind and before you encircle me
> and rest your hand upon me.
6 Such knowledge is too wonderful for me,
> far too lofty for me to reach.
7 Where can I go from your spirit?
> From your presence, where can I flee?
8 If I ascend to the heavens, you are there;
> if I lie down in Sheol, there you are.
9 If I take the wings of dawn
> and dwell beyond the sea,
10 Even there your hand guides me,
> your right hand holds me fast.
11 If I say, "Surely darkness shall hide me,
> and night shall be my light" –
12 Darkness is not dark for you,
> and night shines as the day.
> Darkness and light are but one.
13 You formed my inmost being;
> you knit me in my mother's womb.
14 I praise you, because I am wonderfully made;
> wonderful are your works![...]
16 Your eyes saw me unformed;
> in your book all are written down;
> my days were shaped, before one came to be.
17 How precious to me are your designs, O God;
> how vast the sum of them!
18 Were I to count them, they would outnumber the sands;
> when I complete them, still you are with me.[...]
23 Probe me, God, know my heart;
> try me, know my thoughts.

[24] See if there is a wicked path in me;
    lead me along an ancient path.

Comment

Verse 23 — "Search me, O God, and know my heart" — resembles the beginning of the psalm, and yet it is much more active. For the psalmist, prayer is not a one-way street. We have a relationship with God, which is constantly changing, because we too are constantly changing. God has to be active, to recognize my heart. As my Creator, God puts his trust in me. He knows all my ways, even those I will take in the future, because He makes this future possible. "Your eyes saw how I came into being, in your book everything was already written down" (verse 16). God's book makes my life possible. Therefore God has his place in my heart, where I feel, love, and suffer.

God also creates the relationships in which I live. They are part of my identity. Through my relationships I have become who I am. In them, love is probably the greatest gift I can give and receive. I have often suffered with people who really mean something to me, I have shared with them not only joy but also a lot of pain. I don't find God in abstract terms, but find Him in my relationships with my relatives and friends.

Suggestions

- The first week has begun. My preparation prayer has been found.
- First I prepare the scene for myself.
- Which verse of the Psalm speaks to me most spontaneously? Why?
- What is the most important thing in life for me?
- What or who determines my life?
- How do I experience my relationships?
- What is my relationship with God?
- What does God mean to me?

Film

The Truman Show
USA 1998, 99 Minutes. Directed by Peter Weir

MEDITATION 2

John 15:12-17

[12] This is my commandment: love one another as I love you. [13] No one has greater love than this, to lay down one's life for one's friends. [14] You are my friends if you do what I command you. [15] I no longer call you slaves, because a slave does not know what his master is doing. I have called you friends, because I have told you everything I have heard from my Father. [16] It was not you who chose me, but I who chose you and appointed you to go and bear fruit that will remain, so that whatever you ask the Father in my name he may give you. [17] This I command you: love one another.

Comment

Most believers feel the same way as the disciples: they think they have decided for Jesus of their own accord and have chosen to follow him. In the gospel, however, it appears exactly the opposite. Through Jesus, we are chosen by the Father. As in Psalm 139, the initiative comes from God, and from Jesus.

After choosing his disciples, Jesus is radically open to them. He holds nothing back. What the Father has revealed to him, he passes on, because the Kingdom of God comes into the world through us. It has begun when we respect Jesus's commandment: "Love one another." Three words only, but in them everything is contained. Furthermore, Jesus does not stop at a verbal commandment. He will carry it out on the cross: "There is no greater love than when one gives his life for his friends."

Our hearts know when we do not love, when we are disrespectful, greedy, and hard-hearted. Then there is also no "Kingdom of God," because love is not present. Jesus says in the Sermon on the Mount: "By their fruits you will know them." We may say whatever we like, but the decisive criterion remains our concrete action. We will be judged according to that. What will remain of us in this world? Only the one who acts like Jesus will see his fruit remain.

Suggestions

- First I prepare the scene for myself.
- Do I know that I am chosen by God, by Jesus?
- Do I feel God's love in my life? How do I react to it?
- If I give love, will I be given love in my life?
- When was I disrespectful, greedy, and hard-hearted? Whom have I treated unkindly?
- What "fruit" do I bear in my life?

Film

Gran Torino
USA, Germany, Australia 2008, 116 Min. Directed by Clint Eastwood

MEDITATION 3

Jeremiah 29:11-14

[11] For I know well the plans I have in mind for you — oracle of the LORD — plans for your welfare and not for woe, so as to give you a future of hope. [12] When you call me, and come and pray to me, I will listen to you. [13] When you look for me, you will find me. Yes, when you seek me with all your heart, [14] I will let you find me — oracle of the LORD.

Comment

The prophet Jeremiah is convinced that God has a plan for every human being. God gives us a future of hope and he can be found even now, since he listens when we pray with all our heart. The heart is a traditional image for the human encounter with God, who meets me existentially. "If the heart could think, it would stand still" in silent adoration, says Fernando Pessoa.

Deeper than reflection, deeper than doubt, is this experience that determines the life of the prophet, even if he also knows defeat and failure. Often we invest a lot of energy in certain projects that end in a blind alley, due to our "short-sightedness." We have to let go of some things in order to make room for new ones.

"I have a dream," said Martin Luther King when he began his famous speech. What are or were my dreams? Which ones have been fulfilled? And if they were shattered by reality, have I seen new opportunities grow out of them?

Suggestions

- First I prepare the scene for myself.
- "Everything begins with longing," writes Nelly Sachs. What are my longings? Do I have a motto for my life?
- Does God have any plans for me? Am I following them? Have I drawn up a plan for my life?
- If my plans fail, how do I deal with the failure?
- Can I confide my frailty, my injuries to a friend? Do I talk about them with God?
- For Jeremiah, praying with all his heart is natural. Have I lost my heart? Have I "lost" God?
- What were some particularly painful experiences in my life? Which ones have been transformed by the experience of God's love?
- We do not live alone. I am often dependent on others. How have people changed my life? How do I transform the lives of others?

Film

Three Colors: Blue – Trois Couleurs: Blue
France, Poland 1993, 98 Minutes. Directed by Krzysztof Kieślowski

MEDITATION 4

Genesis 3:1-24

[1] Now the snake was the most cunning of all the wild animals that the Lord God had made. He asked the woman, "Did God really say, 'You shall not eat from any of the trees in the garden'?" [2] The woman answered the snake: "We may eat of the fruit of the trees in the garden; [3] it is only about the fruit of the tree in the middle of the garden that God said, 'You shall not eat it [...], or else you will die.'" [4] But the snake said to the woman: "You certainly will not die! [5] God knows well that when you eat of it your eyes will be opened and you will be like gods, who know good and evil." [6] The woman saw that the tree was good for food [...]. So she took some of its fruit and ate it; and she also gave some to her husband, who was with her, and he ate it. [7] Then the eyes of both of them were opened, and they knew that they were naked[...]

[8] When they heard the sound of the Lord God walking about in the garden [...], the man and his wife hid themselves [...]. [9] The Lord God then called to the man and asked him: Where are you? [10] He answered, "I heard you in the garden; but I was afraid, because I was naked, so I hid." [11] Then God asked: Who told you that you were naked? Have you eaten from the tree of which I had forbidden you to eat? [12] The man replied, "The woman whom you put here with me — she gave me fruit from the tree, so I ate it." [13] The Lord God then asked the woman: What is this you have done? The woman answered, "The snake tricked me, so I ate it."

[14] Then the Lord God said to the snake:

> Because you have done this,
> cursed are you [...].
> On your belly you shall crawl,
> and dust you shall eat
> all the days of your life.
> [15] I will put enmity between you and the woman,
> and between your offspring and hers;
> They will strike at your head,
> while you strike at their heel.

[16] To the woman he said:

> I will intensify your toil in childbearing;
> in pain you shall bring forth children.
> Yet your urge shall be for your husband,
> and he shall rule over you.

¹⁷ To the man he said: Because you listened to your wife and ate from the tree about which I commanded you, You shall not eat from it,
    Cursed is the ground because of you![...].
    ¹⁸ Thorns and thistles it shall bear for you [...].
    ¹⁹ By the sweat of your brow
        you shall eat bread,
    Until you return to the ground,
        from which you were taken;
    For you are dust,
        and to dust you shall return.
²⁰ The man gave his wife the name "Eve," because she was the mother of all the living. [...]
²² Then the Lord God said: See! The man has become like one of us, knowing good and evil! Now, what if he also reaches out his hand to take fruit from the tree of life, and eats of it and lives forever? ²³ The Lord God therefore banished him from the garden of Eden, to till the ground from which he had been taken. ²⁴ He expelled the man, stationing the cherubim and the fiery revolving sword east of the garden of Eden, to guard the way to the tree of life.

Comment

Why did God forbid eating from this tree in the first place? Should God not have known that it was only a matter of time before Adam and Eve would eat from it? After all, the forbidden irritates us much more than what is permitted. If God knew their disobedience ahead of time, free will must have been a characteristic of paradise from the very beginning, far more so than material carefreeness. God could also have created puppets — but how can someone really love, unless it is voluntary? God wanted the highest form of love, and there is no other way to have it. Intensity and fulfillment can only be experienced when we are allowed to choose, when we can freely decide for or against something. We also have to live with the consequences of our choices, which include our transgressions. We are responsible for what we do. However, in the end God has the last word. If we take the words of Jesus seriously, we can trust in the divine mercy that is beyond our imagination.

Suggestions

- First I prepare the scene for myself.
- How free am I actually? And for what do I use the freedom I have?
- We find it easy and most convenient to shift the blame onto others. Children play this game excellently: She started it! Adults also like to shirk their responsibilities. And it is far more painful when one is the victim of an accusation. Have I experienced both sides? How did I feel in each case?
- It is often not easy to take the first step to reform. People who are capable of doing so improve their environment and their relationships. Can I take the first step? In which situations could I not?

Film

East of Eden
USA 1955, 115 Minutes. Directed by Elia Kazan

MEDITATION 5

Matthew 8:1-4

[1] When Jesus came down from the mountain, great crowds followed him. [2] And then a leper approached, did him homage, and said, "Lord, if you wish, you can make me clean." [3] He stretched out his hand, touched him, and said, "I will do it. Be made clean." His leprosy was cleansed immediately. [4] Then Jesus said to him, "See that you tell no one, but go show yourself to the priest, and offer the gift that Moses prescribed; that will be proof for them."

Comment

It was certainly not easy for the sick man to address Jesus in front of the whole crowd. How great his desperation must have been! And the people must have retreated for fear that they themselves might become unclean. Not so Jesus, who is not evasive. To the astonishment of all, he even touches the sick person. Jesus is deeply moved by the trust placed in him: "If you will it, I will be clean," says the leper. The basic trust in Jesus changes everything in the life of the sick person in one fell swoop. If he was previously outcast and lonely, he can now move again freely within his family and society.

Jesus invites us to entrust to him what we desire. When he asks in certain healing stories, "What shall I do for you?", this is by no means meant rhetorically, but speaks to the person in his heart.

Jesus's behavior after the healing is also remarkable. He does not want to publicize it by traveling through the talk shows on television, if there had been such a thing at that time. The sick person should only perform the prescribed ritual in the temple, to thank God for the healing.

Suggestions

- First I prepare the scene for myself.
- When I put myself in the situation of the sick person, would I have the courage to confide in Jesus in public? To ask Jesus to heal me? To have my whole life, all my relationships changed?
- "Necessity teaches to pray," says a proverb. Does God only exist for me when I feel bad?
- When I look at my relationships: Which one is the most important one of all for me?
- Are my relationships bogged down? Do I isolate myself?
- Do I have the courage to end relationships that are not good for me?
- Jesus fundamentally changes the constellation of relationships by making the sick person "socially acceptable." Do I know a similar change in my life from loneliness to community?
- If Jesus asked me: "What shall I do for you?" how would I answer?

Film

Four Minutes – Vier Minuten
Germany 2006, 111 Minutes. Directed by Chris Kraus

MEDITATION 6

John 8:1-11

[1] Jesus went to the Mount of Olives. [2] But early in the morning he arrived again in the temple area, and all the people started coming to him, and he sat down and taught them. [3] Then the scribes and the Pharisees brought a woman who had been caught in adultery and made her stand in the middle. [4] They said to him, "Teacher, this woman was caught in the very act of committing adultery. [5] Now in the law, Moses commanded us to stone such women. So what do you say?" [6] They said this to test him, so that they could have some charge to bring against him. Jesus bent down and began to write on the ground with his finger. [7] But when they continued asking him, he straightened up and said to them, "Let the one among you who is without sin be the first to throw a stone at her." [8] Again he bent down and wrote on the ground. [9] And in response, they went away one by one, beginning with the elders. So he was left alone with the woman before him. [10] Then Jesus straightened up and said to her, "Woman, where are they? Has no one condemned you?" [11] She replied, "No one, sir." Then Jesus said, "Neither do I condemn you. Go, [and] from now on do not sin any more."

Comment

Wherever he goes, Jesus heals people and preaches mercy. Many of the scribes and Pharisees may still remember the parable of the lost son. From their perspective, Jesus is trapped: either he contradicts what he teaches about mercy, or he violates the law of Moses. But Jesus eludes their logic by saying: "Let the one among you who is without sin be the first to throw a stone at her." Those who are quickest to understand him, go away first. Finally, Jesus does not judge the woman, but invites her to a new beginning.

It is easier to criticize others, to condemn and judge them. But conversely, we also experience that we are criticized, that others judge us. Jesus taught us: "Judge not, and you also will not be judged. Condemn not, and you will not be condemned. Forgive each other's guilt, then you too will be forgiven."

Suggestions

- First I prepare the scene for myself.
- Do I experience rejection and condemnation in my life?
- Am I sometimes too quick to judge others?
- Do I find it easy to forgive others?
- Where has forgiveness or mercy been given to me?
- Where have I practiced mercy?

Film

12 Angry Men
USA 1957, 95 Minutes. Directed by Sidney Lumet

MEDITATION 7

Matthew 8:5-13

[5] When he entered Capernaum, a centurion approached him and appealed to him, [6] saying, "Lord, my servant is lying at home paralyzed, suffering dreadfully." [7] He said to him, "I will come and cure him." [8] The centurion said in reply, "Lord, I am not worthy to have you enter under my roof; only say the word and my servant will be healed. [9] For I too am a person subject to authority, with soldiers subject to me. And I say to one, 'Go,' and he goes; and to another, 'Come here,' and he comes; and to my slave, 'Do this,' and he does it." [10] When Jesus heard this, he was amazed and said to those following him, "Amen, I say to you, in no one in Israel have I found such faith. [11] I say to you, many will come from the east and the west, and will recline with Abraham, Isaac, and Jacob at the banquet in the kingdom of heaven, [12] but the children of the kingdom will be driven out into the outer darkness, where there will be wailing and grinding of teeth." [13] And Jesus said to the centurion, "You may go; as you have believed, let it be done for you." And at that very hour [his] servant was healed.

Comment

Not very often is Jesus reported to be astonished. But the faith of this Roman is unusual. We know his words only too well, since we speak them in every Eucharistic celebration before Communion. The liturgy invites us to surprise Jesus, by believing as firmly as the Roman centurion did. Perhaps we could say something a little more positive: "Lord, make me worthy that you enter under my roof. Speak one word and my soul will be healed."

To be saved, a single word is enough. Often there are situations in which I am not able to utter this one redeeming word, although I know what it is. I am paralyzed by the fear of the consequences, the fear to show myself vulnerable. It is exactly in such situations that I should participate in the healing power of Jesus.

Suggestions

- First I prepare the scene for myself.
- When I look at my life, do I see many situations that I could have changed with the centurion's faith?
- Who am I responsible for? Do I stand up adequately for this person?
- Do I dare to amaze Jesus like the centurion?
- Which "one word" do I wish for?
- Am I satisfied with my life so far? Where was joy, where suffering, where failure, where healing? What do I want to change? The invitation to the sacrament of reconciliation is always present.

Film

The Reader
USA, Germany 2008, 124 Minutes. Directed by Stephen Daldry

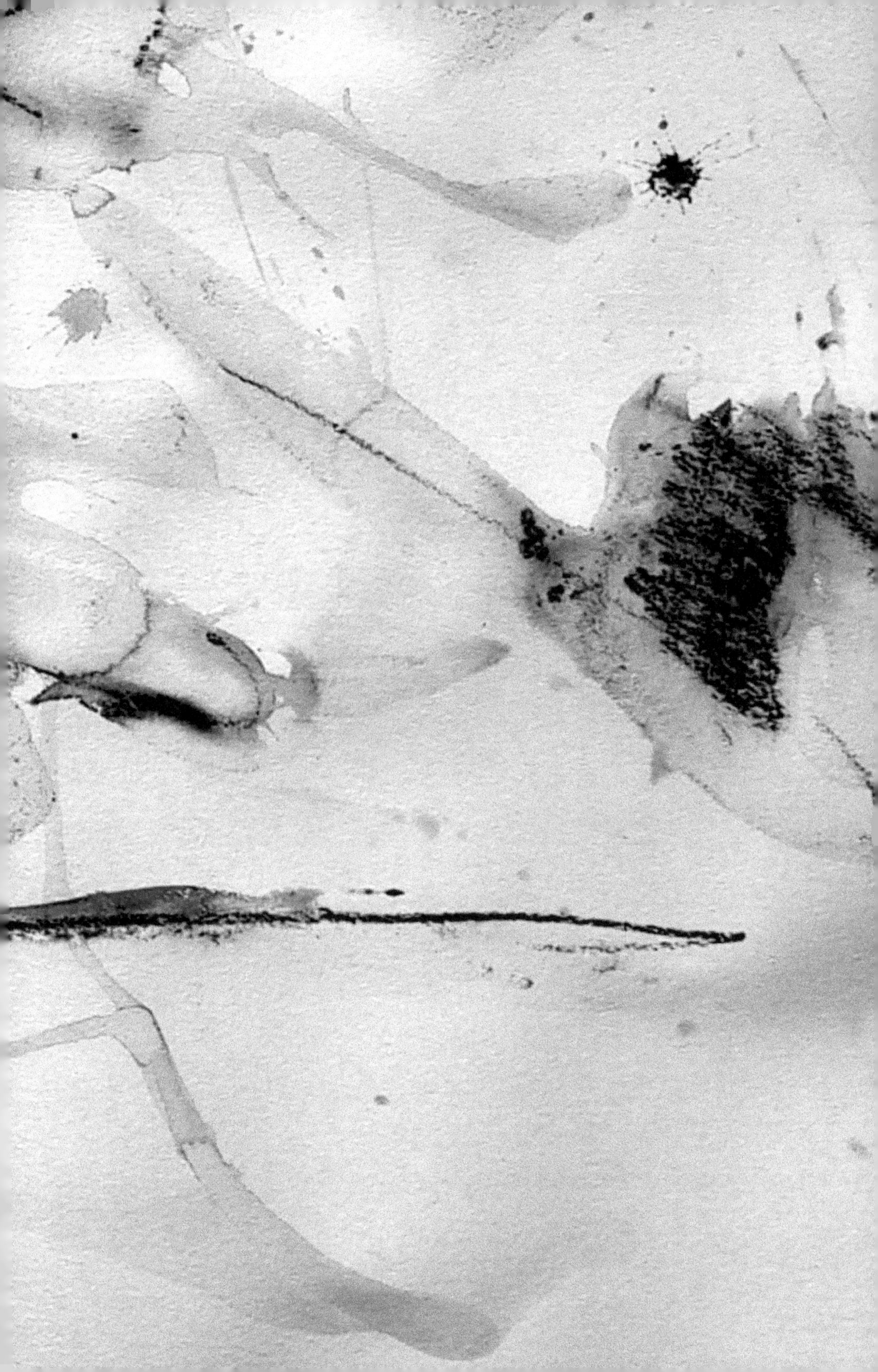

SECOND WEEK:
LIFE OF JESUS

Socrates says: "An unexamined life is not worth living." Behind this is the question of the standard by which I judge myself in my life. What values and ideals do I have? Often the answer is: What you spend the most time and money on, that is your highest value. It is certainly worthwhile to think about this. However, a skewed picture can emerge, because we are not always free to choose what we do and how much effort we put into it. Whether I like what I do, on the other hand, is also relevant to the question of my highest value. What ultimately motivates me to do something goes deeper than time or money, or liking it.

Every person is looking for autonomy, competence, and affiliation. I would like to decide for myself; I would like to be able to do something particularly well; and would like not to live it alone, but in relationship. The human will is a double entity. I may want something — career, wealth, happiness, relationships, etc. — but then I can ask myself if I really want what I want. If I can answer this question in the affirmative, that is, if I know what I really want, it leads me to true freedom, and I recognize my "true self," as Sören Kierkegaard called it.

However, the decisive question still remains open: How do I find out what I really want? How do I avoid being mistaken about my true self? How do I get out of my pure self-centeredness? Spiritually asked: What is the will of God for me and my life? God's will for me, Ignatius is convinced, is revealed by the contemplation of the life of Jesus. That is the key for the way I want to live my life. Jesus did not preach about an abstract God, the "unmoved mover" (Aristotle), but the Father who loves man without reservation. God loves us as no man loves or can love. Even if the whole world condemns us, God restores us like the prodigal son. "God is closer to our self than we ourselves are," says Augustine.

The second week is often seen as the center of the retreat, because here is where the person praying is invited to make a choice. How can I know God's will for me, in order to choose it? Ignatius himself gives three criteria. First: What I choose must be good in itself. Second: Does it give me inner peace (comfort) in my soul? And third: Does it serve other people? My decision — whether I stand before a concrete choice like partnership or religious vocation, or whether I want to confirm myself in the choice I have already made — is about self-realization. For the philosopher Alfred North Whitehead, self-realization is the heart of reality: "What is real realizes itself, and what realizes itself is real." In the end, my longings express themselves in what I allow to become reality. The crucial question of this week: Where do I hear the call of Jesus in my life? What self-realization does he call me to?

MEDITATION 1

John 1:1-12

¹ In the beginning was the Word,
and the Word was with God,
and the Word was God.
² He was in the beginning with God.
³ All things came to be through him,
and without him nothing came to be.
What came to be ⁴ through him was life,
and this life was the light of the human race;
⁵ the light shines in the darkness,
and the darkness has not overcome it.

⁶ A man named John was sent from God. ⁷ He came for testimony, to testify to the light, so that all might believe through him. ⁸ He was not the light, but came to testify to the light. ⁹ The true light, which enlightens everyone, was coming into the world.

¹⁰ He was in the world,
and the world came to be through him,
but the world did not know him.
¹¹ He came to what was his own,
but his own people did not accept him.

¹² But to those who did accept him he gave power to become children of God, to those who believe in his name.

Comment

The gospel of John is the latest of the gospels, with its prologue more like poetry than a strict dogmatic explanation. According to the prologue, life begins in God, who creates becoming and form. God guarantees that the world does not sink into chaos, that there is order and creativity, continuing into a future. His light shines in every life that has been created.

Before God sends His Son into this world, He calls John as a witness who prepares the way for Jesus. This is John the Baptist, who lives in the desert, feeding on locusts and honey. He attracts people, and many follow his call to repentance and are baptized by him as a sign of this. Because he criticizes those in power (Herod and his wife Herodias), he pays with his life. Like Jesus himself, John experiences acceptance and rejection. But his main function is to testify to the true light, present in Jesus. Whoever accepts it becomes a child of God, concludes the first part of the prologue.

Belonging to the children of God is open to all people. Every person is invited to make an active decision: I can reject God, or I can accept God. The decision for God gives me the power to be a child of God. This is not the power of the powerful. As a child of God I live without hidden intentions and resentments, but rather with curiosity, joy, and gratitude.

Suggestions

- First I prepare the scene for myself.
- Do I feel myself to be a daughter, or a son of God? What does being a child of God mean to me?
- Is my relationship with God like a child's relationship with its parents? Do I feel His motherly and fatherly concern for me?
- What does God mean for me?
- Do I reject certain images of God? Why?
- Do I experience rejection or acceptance when I confess Jesus?
- Do I bear witness to Jesus's coming, as John did?

Film

The Gospel of John
Canada, Great Britain 2003, 171 Minutes. Directed by Philip Saville

MEDITATION 2

Luke 1:26-38

[26] In the sixth month, the angel Gabriel was sent from God to a town of Galilee called Nazareth, [27] to a virgin betrothed to a man named Joseph, of the house of David, and the virgin's name was Mary. [28] And coming to her, he said, "Hail, favored one! The Lord is with you." [29] But she was greatly troubled at what was said and pondered what sort of greeting this might be. [30] Then the angel said to her, "Do not be afraid, Mary, for you have found favor with God. [31] Behold, you will conceive in your womb and bear a son, and you shall name him Jesus. [32] He will be great and will be called Son of the Most High, and the Lord God will give him the throne of David his father, [33] and he will rule over the house of Jacob forever, and of his kingdom there will be no end." [34] But Mary said to the angel, "How can this be, since I have no relations with a man?" [35] And the angel said to her in reply, "The holy Spirit will come upon you, and the power of the Most High will overshadow you. Therefore the child to be born will be called holy, the Son of God. [36] And behold, Elizabeth, your relative, has also conceived a son in her old age, and this is the sixth month for her who was called barren; [37] for nothing will be impossible for God." [38] Mary said, "Behold, I am the handmaid of the Lord. May it be done to me according to your word." Then the angel departed from her.

Comment

Salvation history begins with an announcement. Mary shall conceive a child by the Holy Spirit. Mary may be young, but she is not naive. She asks the angel: how can this be? But above all, a decision is demanded of Mary.

Were the scene filmed from the perspective of heaven, one would now be able to hear a pin drop, since all would be anxiously hoping for Mary's "yes."

God does not compel us humans, but rather invites us to come out of our comfort zone and daily routine. Mary's brave acceptance of that "crazy" announcement (without any "ifs," "ands," or "buts") begins a turning point in human history. God becomes human — not on the red carpet but as a helpless little child.

The gospels tell us little about the childhood of Jesus. But at least we know about Joseph, Mary's fiancé and later her husband. He says not a single word in the gospels. Luke does not tell us how he accepted the message of the angel; in Matthew 1:18-25, he receives his own message from an angel, in a dream.

In the adult life of Jesus God does not intervene directly, although he often intervenes in the early days by sending dreams to Joseph, to keep the child and his family from harm.

As with all children, parents are also important for Jesus as he grows up. From them he received an understanding of God and the world, even if he later outgrew it in his own special way. Above all, however, he received from them love.

Suggestions

- First I prepare the scene for myself.
- What important decisions have I made in my life?
- Why did I choose one thing rather than another? Would I make the same choice today?
- Can I give God an unconditional "yes," like Mary? What consequences does that have for me?
- What is my calling? How and when has God called me in my life?
- My faith has changed as I grew up. Do I still cling to certain ideas of my childhood faith? In what respect have I outgrown them, like Jesus?

Film

The Gospel according to Matthew – Il Vangelo Secondo Matteo
Italy 1964. 183 Minutes. Directed by Pier Paolo Pasolini.

MEDITATION 3

Luke 2:25-38

25 Now there was a man in Jerusalem whose name was Simeon. This man was righteous and devout, awaiting the consolation of Israel, and the holy Spirit was upon him. 26 It had been revealed to him by the holy Spirit that he should not see death before he had seen the Messiah of the Lord. 27 He came in the Spirit into the temple; and when the parents brought in the child Jesus to perform the custom of the law in regard to him, 28 he took him into his arms and blessed God, saying:

> 29 "Now, Master, you may let your servant go
>
>> in peace, according to your word,
>
> 30 for my eyes have seen your salvation,
>
>> 31 which you prepared in sight of all the peoples,
>
> 32 a light for revelation to the Gentiles,
>
>> and glory for your people Israel."

33 The child's father and mother were amazed at what was said about him; 34 and Simeon blessed them and said to Mary his mother, "Behold, this child is destined for the fall and rise of many in Israel, and to be a sign that will be contradicted 35 (and you yourself a sword will pierce) so that the thoughts of many hearts may be revealed." 36 There was also a prophetess, Anna, the daughter of Phanuel, of the tribe of Asher. She was advanced in years, having lived seven years with her husband after her marriage, 37 and then as a widow until she was eighty-four. She never left the temple, but worshiped night and day with fasting and prayer. 38 And coming forward at that very time, she gave thanks to God and spoke about the child to all who were awaiting the redemption of Jerusalem.

Comment

Hardly any other scene of Jesus's childhood will be remembered by his parents as much as this one. The praise of Simeon and Anna makes Joseph and Mary at first proud and happy, but in the end they turn pale, because the prophecy ends with a shock. How can Jesus be the "salvation of the nations" and also "the sign that is contradicted"? Contradiction does not sound positive — what does it really mean?

As if that were not enough, Simeon also says to Mary: "But a sword will pierce your soul." It could hardly be more drastic. What will Joseph and Mary have thought? They probably didn't feel like celebrating anymore.

The evangelists do not tell much about the first thirty years of Jesus's life. Most of it remains hidden. But Luke tells us one more scene, in which the temple again plays an important role. Since the temple contained the ark of the covenant with the tablets of the law of Moses, it was the holiest place of the Jews.

Joseph and Mary are on their way home to Nazareth after the Passover celebration and assume that their twelve-year-old son is on his way home with his relatives. But Jesus remained in Jerusalem. After three days of intensive searching, they find him in the temple, talking to the teachers, listening attentively to them, and asking clever questions. Upset, Mary rebukes him: "Child, how could you do this to us? Your father and I searched for you in fear." Jesus answers: "Why did you seek me? Did you not know that I must be in what belongs to my father?" And again the parents do not understand exactly what is meant, although this time it is their own son who speaks. However, as the text goes on to say, "his mother kept everything that had happened in her heart."

Luke does not tell us how Jesus spent his youth; instead, he condenses the story into a single sentence: "But Jesus grew up and his wisdom increased and he found favor with God and men."

Suggestions

- First I prepare the scene for myself.
- To which places am I attracted? Why? What are holy places for me?
- How do I imagine the young Jesus?
- Jesus distances himself from his parents. For him the experience of the holy, the divine father in the temple, is more important than obedience to his parents. Do I know similar situations?
- How do I experience my parents, my family in relation to my life path?
- The young Jesus feels his calling and shows this by staying in "his father's house." What do I feel as my calling? What visible signs are there?

Film

Vitus

Switzerland 2005, 123 Minutes. Directed by Fredi M. Murer

MEDITATION 4

Luke 4:1-13

[1] Filled with the holy Spirit, Jesus returned from the Jordan and was led by the Spirit into the desert [2] for forty days, to be tempted by the devil. He ate nothing during those days, and when they were over he was hungry. [3] The devil said to him, "If you are the Son of God, command this stone to become bread." [4] Jesus answered him, "It is written, 'One does not live by bread alone.'" [5] Then he took him up and showed him all the kingdoms of the world in a single instant. [6] The devil said to him, "I shall give to you all this power and their glory; for it has been handed over to me, and I may give it to whomever I wish. [7] All this will be yours, if you worship me." [8] Jesus said to him in reply, "It is written:

> 'You shall worship the Lord, your God,
>
>> and him alone shall you serve.'"

[9] Then he led him to Jerusalem, made him stand on the parapet of the temple, and said to him, "If you are the Son of God, throw yourself down from here, [10] for it is written:

> 'He will command his angels concerning you,
>
>> to guard you,'

[11] and:

> 'With their hands they will support you,
>
>> lest you dash your foot against a stone.'"

[12] Jesus said to him in reply, "It also says, 'You shall not put the Lord, your God, to the test.'" [13] When the devil had finished every temptation, he departed from him for a time.

Comment

What happened when Jesus left home and went into the desert? To go into the desert alone is not only to go into loneliness. You also have to feed yourself and above all you need water to survive. What experiences might Jesus have had during the forty days? The Bible tells us about three of them — the three temptations. All three concern the first commandment: "I am the Lord your God. You shall have no other gods beside me! You shall not make for yourselves any idol to worship." God alone counts, not the deification of earthly power and the dependence that it brings. Freedom is a gift of God. It can be experienced as freedom of choice, and above all as inner freedom from earthly dependence.

Whoever can turn stones into bread can also rule the world with "panem et circenses" (bread and games in the circus). Jesus would have the ability to do this. But he refuses to use it, even for himself, because only God can give the true bread, the true security.

Even later it is very strange for his environment that Jesus does not make his ability to heal the sick and the possessed into a profitable business. But the salvation of God is free. It can neither be bought nor earned. Therefore Jesus escapes the well-known dynamics of wealth, honor, pride, and vanity. With his talent, he could have become very rich and famous throughout Judea and far beyond. But as manager of a healing empire, he would have found it almost impossible to speak out for ordinary people, and for those on the margins. After all, he would have had to take care of his public reputation in order not to harm the business; every appearance of the famous healer would have been carefully observed. True pastoral care must be free from this dynamic. Rather, it is necessary to give generously with all one's heart and remain humble.

Wealth can easily make you lonely, because you cannot buy real friends. And there is always the nagging doubt whether people love you only because of your wealth or for your own sake.

Suggestions

- First I prepare the scene for myself.
- Do I meet Jesus in the desert? What is my relationship to him?
- Do I get into conversation with Jesus? What do I ask?
- Desert is a place of silence and solitude. Where do I experience this in my life?
- Do I know the dynamics of wealth, honor, pride and vanity? How do I behave towards them?
- Do I make myself dependent on the judgment and opinions of others?
- What are my three temptations?

Film

The Devil's Advocate
USA 1997, 144 Minutes. Directed by Taylor Hackford

MEDITATION 5

Luke 4:14-30

[14] Jesus returned to Galilee in the power of the Spirit, and news of him spread throughout the whole region. [15] He taught in their synagogues and was praised by all.

[16] He came to Nazareth, where he had grown up, and went according to his custom into the synagogue on the sabbath day. He stood up to read [17] and was handed a scroll of the prophet Isaiah. He unrolled the scroll and found the passage where it was written:

> [18] "The Spirit of the Lord is upon me,
>
>> because he has anointed me
>>
>>> to bring glad tidings to the poor.
>
> He has sent me to proclaim liberty to captives
>
>> and recovery of sight to the blind,
>>
>>> to let the oppressed go free,
>
>> [19] and to proclaim a year acceptable to the Lord."

[20] Rolling up the scroll, he handed it back to the attendant and sat down, and the eyes of all in the synagogue looked intently at him. [21] He said to them, "Today this scripture passage is fulfilled in your hearing." [22] And all spoke highly of him and were amazed at the gracious words that came from his mouth. They also asked, "Isn't this the son of Joseph?" [23] He said to them, "Surely you will quote me this proverb, 'Physician, cure yourself,' and say, 'Do here in your native place the things that we heard were done in Capernaum.'" [24] And he said, "Amen, I say to you, no prophet is accepted in his own native place. [25] Indeed, I tell you, there were many widows in Israel in the days of Elijah when the sky was closed for three and a half years and a severe famine spread over the entire land. [26] It was to none of these that Elijah was sent, but only to a widow in Zarephath in the land of Sidon. [27] Again, there were many lepers in Israel during the time of Elisha the prophet; yet not one of them was cleansed, but only Naaman the Syrian." [28] When the people in the synagogue heard this, they were all filled with fury. [29] They rose up, drove him out of the town, and led him to the brow of the hill on which their town had been built, to hurl him down headlong. [30] But he passed through the midst of them and went away.

Comment

Jesus is back in his home town. All eyes are on him. His message is clear: he has come to heal what is wounded, to bring freedom to the oppressed, and to transform suffering into life. This is the message of the Kingdom of God, and it has begun here and now. It is an offer to us. We can refuse it or share in it. For God's salvation we need our openness, our "yes" to God. That means it is our decision and our responsibility.

Often our talents are more appreciated by our friends than by our family. Jesus has to have this bitter experience too. "A prophet is not without honor except in his native place and among his own kin and in his own house," as he puts it in a nutshell. In the synagogue, the atmosphere turns into open hostility at the end. Jesus remains the strongest in this threatening situation; he leaves at the right moment.

When Jesus leaves his home, his wanderings make him sensitive to the needs of others, and he finds new friends. Being on the road always means learning new things. Jesus's public ministry is also a time of learning for himself. The encounter with the Samaritan woman at Jacob's well shows him that he is not only sent into the world for a chosen people, but for all people. Leaving familiar surroundings may hurt, but departure is essential so that I can open myself to new experiences. The more I let go, the more I am given.

Suggestions

- First I prepare the scene for myself.
- Do I confess the message of Jesus? What hinders me, what encourages me?
- The Kingdom of God needs my assistance. What can I do?
- Whom do I give recognition to? Whom do I deny it to?
- Do I experience rejection? How do I react to this?
- What new experiences in my life would not have been possible without my "letting go" of familiar things?

Film

Whale Rider

Germany, New Zealand 2002, 101 Minutes. Directed by Niki Caro

MEDITATION 6

Luke 5:1-11

[1] While the crowd was pressing in on Jesus and listening to the word of God, he was standing by the Lake of Gennesaret. [2] He saw two boats there alongside the lake; the fishermen had disembarked and were washing their nets. [3] Getting into one of the boats, the one belonging to Simon, he asked him to put out a short distance from the shore. Then he sat down and taught the crowds from the boat. [4] After he had finished speaking, he said to Simon, "Put out into deep water and lower your nets for a catch." [5] Simon said in reply, "Master, we have worked hard all night and have caught nothing, but at your command I will lower the nets." [6] When they had done this, they caught a great number of fish and their nets were tearing. [7] They signaled to their partners in the other boat to come to help them. They came and filled both boats so that they were in danger of sinking. [8] When Simon Peter saw this, he fell at the knees of Jesus and said, "Depart from me, Lord, for I am a sinful man." [9] For astonishment at the catch of fish they had made seized him and all those with him, [10] and likewise James and John, the sons of Zebedee, who were partners of Simon. Jesus said to Simon, "Do not be afraid; from now on you will be catching men." [11] When they brought their boats to the shore, they left everything and followed him.

Comment

Common to all vocation stories in the gospels is that the initiative comes from Jesus. The disciples do not decide to follow Jesus of their own accord. He invites them to leave everything and become "fishers of men" for the Kingdom of God. And they simply follow him. The gospels report no long discussions and no dithering. Jesus must have had a simply convincing way, which made all this unnecessary.

This is difficult for us humans today to understand. We want to determine and control our lives ourselves: for example, I am the one who chooses my profession or studies. I have an allergic reaction to heteronomy, to being ruled by someone else.

What at first glance appears to be a contradiction, however, need not be one. The initiative may well come from Jesus, but I must then agree to accept his offer. And I can also reject it.

When I follow Jesus, there are serious consequences. "Do not think that I have come to bring peace to the earth. I have not come to bring peace, but the sword. For I came to divide the son from his father, and the daughter from her mother, and the daughter-in-law from her mother-in-law."

The sword is not only a tool of violence; it is also a tool that cuts sharply and precisely. Separated from their former ways, Simon Peter, James, and John begin a new chapter in their lives, full of uncertainty, but with Jesus's promise: "He who receives you receives me, and he who receives me receives him who sent me."

Suggestions

- First I prepare the scene for myself.
- Do all initiatives come from me alone? Do I hear the call of Jesus, the call of God in my life?
- Am I ready to follow Jesus radically? What are the consequences?
- Who is Jesus for me?
- Do I have a faith appropriate to my age? Do I know radical new beginnings in my life of faith? What opportunities, what new experiences were associated with them?
- Jesus wants to share his experience and power with us. Where can I learn about Jesus's abilities?

Film

The Mission
Great Britain 1986, 125 Minutes. Directed by Roland Joffé

MEDITATION 7

Mark 10:17-27

[17] As he was setting out on a journey, a man ran up, knelt down before him, and asked him, "Good teacher, what must I do to inherit eternal life?" [18] Jesus answered him, "Why do you call me good? No one is good but God alone. [19] You know the commandments: 'You shall not kill; you shall not commit adultery; you shall not steal; you shall not bear false witness; you shall not defraud; honor your father and your mother.'" [20] He replied and said to him, "Teacher, all of these I have observed from my youth." [21] Jesus, looking at him, loved him and said to him, "You are lacking in one thing. Go, sell what you have, and give to [the] poor and you will have treasure in heaven; then come, follow me." [22] At that statement his face fell, and he went away sad, for he had many possessions.

[23] Jesus looked around and said to his disciples, "How hard it is for those who have wealth to enter the kingdom of God!" [24] The disciples were amazed at his words. So Jesus again said to them in reply, "Children, how hard it is to enter the kingdom of God! [25] It is easier for a camel to pass through [the] eye of [a] needle than for one who is rich to enter the kingdom of God."

[26] They were exceedingly astonished and said among themselves, "Then who can be saved?" [27] Jesus looked at them and said, "For human beings it is impossible, but not for God. All things are possible for God."

Comment

Something is missing from the young man. He himself cannot (yet) name it. How can he reach his life goal, for which he uses the phrase "eternal life?" At first he can answer Jesus's counter-questions positively, but his heart is still attached to his possessions. The sadness about not being able to let go of possessions has an echo of loneliness. To follow Jesus means to radically renounce everything. Wealth especially seems to be a real challenge. In the Old Testament, wealth and possessions mean that one is blessed by God. And now, all of a sudden, this is no longer true? Even the disciples get scared. Perhaps the eye of the needle just needs to be made bigger? It seems impossible by our standards, but not for God's mercy.

If you have a lot of money, you probably have a treasure — but is it a "permanent" one? How much time and energy it takes to maintain and increase all this wealth! And who benefits from all this? Do you want to be buried as the richest person in the world one day? That would be the inherent dynamic of greed: being rich for the sake of being rich. But perhaps the deficit lies less in wanting to have than in a lack of solidarity with people. Jesus's alternative to wealth is the community. He invites us to this.

Suggestions

- First I prepare the scene for myself.
- What is my life goal?
- What do I use my talents for?
- How much time do I spend "wanting to have" things?
- What does fellowship with Jesus mean to me?
- What prevents me from following Jesus?

Film

Bruce Almighty
USA 2003, 101 Minutes. Directed by Tom Shadyac

MEDITATION 8

John 15:1-8

[1] "I am the true vine, and my Father is the vine grower. [2] He takes away every branch in me that does not bear fruit, and every one that does he prunes so that it bears more fruit. [3] You are already pruned because of the word that I spoke to you. [4] Remain in me, as I remain in you. Just as a branch cannot bear fruit on its own unless it remains on the vine, so neither can you unless you remain in me. [5] I am the vine, you are the branches. Whoever remains in me and I in him will bear much fruit, because without me you can do nothing. [6] Anyone who does not remain in me will be thrown out like a branch and wither; people will gather them and throw them into a fire and they will be burned. [7] If you remain in me and my words remain in you, ask for whatever you want and it will be done for you. [8] By this is my Father glorified, that you bear much fruit and become my disciples."

Comment

A vine can become very powerful. And its branches grow differently: some are more vigorous, others more delicate. Some bear fruit, others do not. Some vines are particularly vigorous — but they do not bear fruit. Still others are withered. For a very good wine to be pressed out later, a vine needs good care. The branches that grow poorly or wither are cut back.

Jesus lives in us. When we follow him and unfold creatively, or live intensively in relationships, there is rich fruit. Sometimes we invest a lot of energy in wrong decisions and projects. Then the vine is strong, but without fruit. We build on what we have been in the past, based on how we have decided. But what we will be has always the chance to produce new fruit. Each vine branch is unique and always stretches out for new development. At the same time it is dependent on the main vine, which provides it with nutrients and life, making the new growth possible. "Where the Spirit of the Lord is, there is freedom," writes St. Paul. Wherever our actions bear rich fruit, there we are connected with Jesus, with God, in a special way.

Jesus promises that if we first care about the Kingdom of God and really follow Him, then we can ask for whatever we want, and it will be given to us. On the other hand, he who cares only for himself withers away. Only he who gives himself away to God will receive and grow.

Perhaps the picture of the vine was a suggestion for the preparatory prayer proposed by Ignatius. He saw that in all the good I do, God works in this world.

Suggestions

- First I prepare the scene for myself.
- Which vine branches in my life are withered?
- Which vine branches in my life bring rich fruit?
- Which vine branches in my life are particularly vigorous, but do not bear fruit?
- Where do I feel a special connection with Jesus?

Film

Dead Poets Society
USA 1988, 128 Minutes. Directed by Peter Weir

THE FIVE FREEDOMS

The freedom
to see and hear what is here
instead of what should be, was, or will be.

The freedom
to say what one feels and thinks,
instead of what one should.

The freedom
to feel what one feels,
instead of what one ought.

The freedom
to ask for what one wants,
instead of always waiting for permission.

The freedom
to take risks in one's own behalf,
instead of choosing to be only "secure" and not
rocking the boat.

Virginia Satir

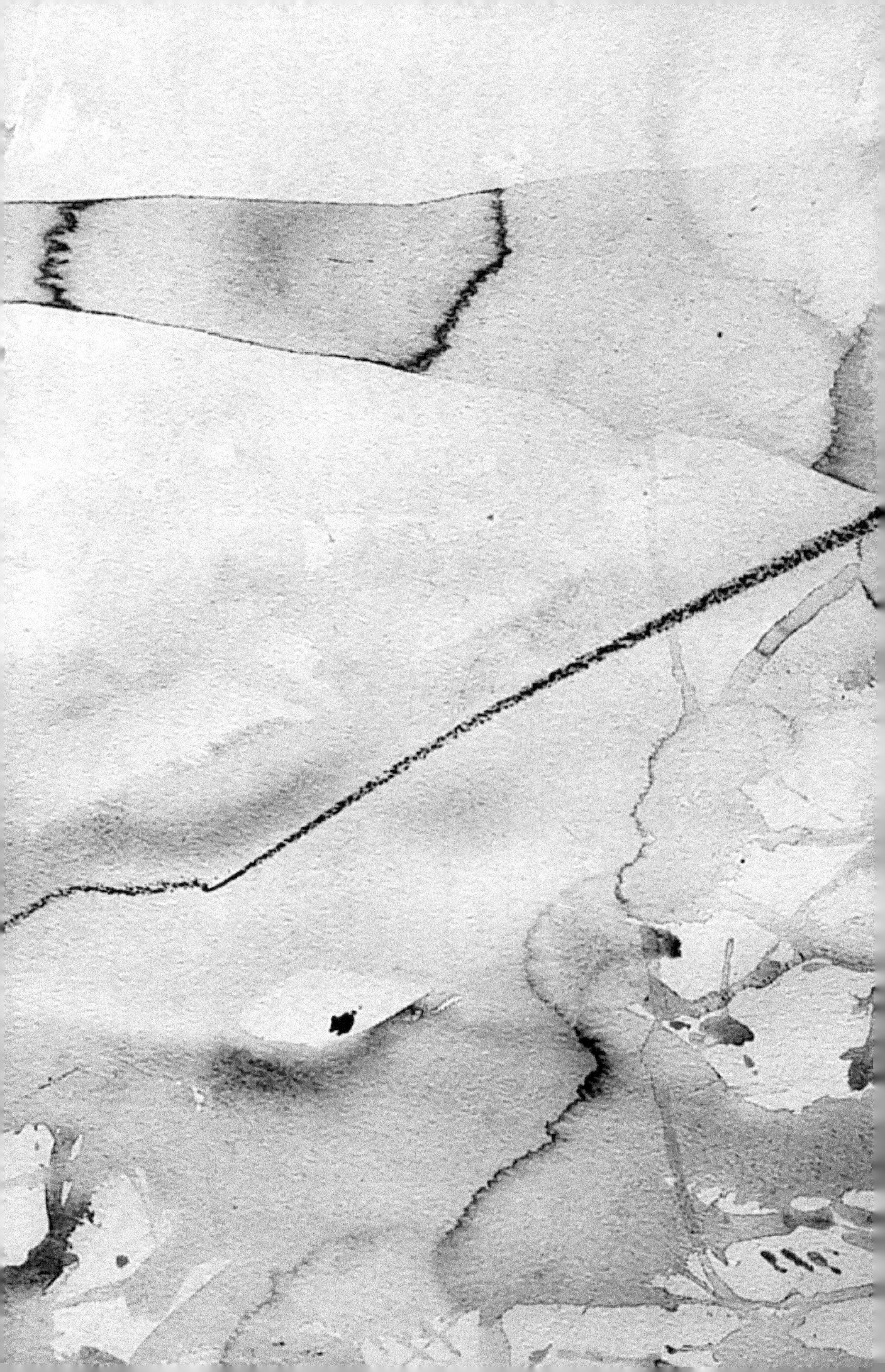

THIRD WEEK: SUFFERING OF JESUS

An essential quality of every human being is the capacity for compassion. Am I capable of making a victim's perspective my own? Even if the suffering of the other person will always remain his own, I can sincerely pity him, comfort him, take him in my arms. And I feel yet another pain, because my own values and ideals have also been wounded by what happened to him. This is the connection to the dynamics of the first week.

In the Old Testament we find the image of the hardened heart. Yahweh promises the Israelites a new heart instead of the old one made of stone — a new heart that can suffer. Ignatius had such a heart; he had the "gift of tears" and wept during spiritual exercises. Whoever weeps knows the purification, relief, and redemption that is connected with it. There is no need for visible tears, because a heart can cry even without them. And we look forward to the time after this valley of tears, when suffering is transformed into new life.

Many people suffer from violence, and this is difficult to deal with. Sometimes repressing memory is the only way to cope with the situation. Anyone who is traumatized should be prepared for what may follow. Without good guidance, the path of recovery becomes arduous, perhaps even dangerous. But when you are no longer overwhelmed by pain and tears, you have regained a large piece of inner freedom. The suffering inflicted on me loses its power and no longer dominates me.

No one seeks suffering or wants to suffer. Nonetheless, mature people can accept their own suffering and transform it. They have reconciled themselves with their fate: for example, by learning to live with an incurable illness. They have a depth and wisdom that healthy people often lack.

MEDITATION 1

Mark 14:1-9

[1] The Passover and the Feast of Unleavened Bread were to take place in two days' time. So the chief priests and the scribes were seeking a way to arrest him by treachery and put him to death. [2] They said, "Not during the festival, for fear that there may be a riot among the people."

[3] When he was in Bethany reclining at table in the house of Simon the leper, a woman came with an alabaster jar of perfumed oil, costly genuine spikenard. She broke the alabaster jar and poured it on his head. [4] There were some who were indignant. "Why has there been this waste of perfumed oil? [5] It could have been sold for more than three hundred days' wages and the money given to the poor." They were infuriated with her. [6] Jesus said, "Let her alone. Why do you make trouble for her? She has done a good thing for me. [7] The poor you will always have with you, and whenever you wish you can do good to them, but you will not always have me. [8] She has done what she could. She has anticipated anointing my body for burial. [9] Amen, I say to you, wherever the gospel is proclaimed to the whole world, what she has done will be told in memory of her."

Comment

Jesus is a guest of Simon in Bethany, a few days before the great feast begins in Jerusalem. When suddenly a woman approaches Jesus and anoints his head, it becomes very quiet. All eyes are on Jesus.

To anoint someone's head means to sanctify him — to place him in God's proximity in a special way. Thus kings, prophets, and priests were anointed; but also the sick and the dead. Jesus lets it happen and rebukes those who scold the woman. They fall silent, highly irritated. What is wrong with Jesus? Didn't they work together tirelessly for the poor and marginalized in the past few years? Why is this no longer true?

Jesus knows that it is only a matter of time before the establishment turns against him by force. The woman seems to be the only one who understands what is really important now — and Jesus can accept it.

Anointing also involves touching, and here we see something seldom seen in the Bible. It is rarely told that Jesus lets someone touch him. Those who did include the woman who suffered from bleeding for years, the other woman who washes his feet with her tears, or Thomas, whom Jesus invites to put his hand into the stigmata. Otherwise it is always Jesus who acts and heals.

But now he seems tired. And the woman senses this. She does not waste unnecessary words, but simply gives Jesus what she can give: the benefit of a loving touch. This says more than a thousand words.

Suggestions

- First I prepare the scene for myself.
- Jesus has sorrow — how would I show him my love?
- Could I allow someone to waste money on me?
- Do I sometimes feel that a touch would be more comforting than words? Do I then dare to give this comfort and take someone in my arms in front of others?
- Every baptized person is anointed with Chrism oil as a sign that she or he has a share in Christ (which literally means the "anointed one"). I am anointed like Jesus to be priest, king, and prophet. What does this mean for me?

Film

The Diving Bell and the Butterfly – Le Scaphandre et le Papillon
France, USA 2007, 112 Minutes. Directed by Julian Schnabel

MEDITATION 2

John 2:13-22

[13]Since the Passover of the Jews was near, Jesus went up to Jerusalem. [14] He found in the temple area those who sold oxen, sheep, and doves, as well as the money-changers seated there. [15] He made a whip out of cords and drove them all out of the temple area, with the sheep and oxen, and spilled the coins of the money-changers and overturned their tables, [16] and to those who sold doves he said, "Take these out of here, and stop making my Father's house a marketplace." [17] His disciples recalled the words of scripture, "Zeal for your house will consume me." [18] At this the Jews answered and said to him, "What sign can you show us for doing this?" [19] Jesus answered and said to them, "Destroy this temple and in three days I will raise it up." [20] The Jews said, "This temple has been under construction for forty-six years, and you will raise it up in three days?" [21] But he was speaking about the temple of his body. [22] Therefore, when he was raised from the dead, his disciples remembered that he had said this, and they came to believe the scripture and the word Jesus had spoken.

Comment

Jesus goes to the temple in Jerusalem, "into the house of his father". He wants to pray, returning once more to the place where he found his home when he was twelve years old. The preparations for the feast have begun. Countless people are crowding in the forecourt of the temple. Amid the noise, a person cannot hear himself speak. Jesus does not manage to find his way through the crowd. And how can one pray in all the bustle and noise? Anger rises in him, and he starts to drive out the merchants and their customers. They are shocked. Who has the authority to do such a thing? They cannot believe their eyes: is this the Jesus they know?

The one who acts there, filled with holy wrath, is not the "dear Jesus" shown in the pious kitsch pictures. As a gentle lamb, he might have complained to the high priests in a well-behaved manner and received in return a mild smile from them. Certainly nothing would have changed. But Jesus is not diplomatic. He does not write a petition; he acts.

Those who are angry and act will not always do everything right, but they let the situation really hit them in the heart. And they have the energy to change something, by trying something new. However, it is more comfortable to never let oneself be carried away by indignation against injustice, and instead to swim in the stream of indifference.

Suggestions

- First I prepare the scene for myself.
- Can I sympathize with Jesus?
- Do I sometimes get angry? About what?
- Does my anger have consequences?
- Do I prefer to take the path of least resistance and adapt my swimming to the current? Since when and why? Have I ever tried to change that?

Film

Jesus of Montreal – Jésus de Montréal

Canada, France 1989, 119 Minutes. Directed by Denys Arcand

MEDITATION 3

John 13:1-17

[1] Before the feast of Passover, Jesus knew that his hour had come to pass from this world to the Father. He loved his own in the world and he loved them to the end. [2] The devil had already induced Judas, son of Simon the Iscariot, to hand him over. So, during supper, [3] fully aware that the Father had put everything into his power and that he had come from God and was returning to God, [4] he rose from supper and took off his outer garments. He took a towel and tied it around his waist. [5] Then he poured water into a basin and began to wash the disciples' feet and dry them with the towel around his waist. [6] He came to Simon Peter, who said to him, "Master, are you going to wash my feet?" [7] Jesus answered and said to him, "What I am doing, you do not understand now, but you will understand later." [8] Peter said to him, "You will never wash my feet." Jesus answered him, "Unless I wash you, you will have no inheritance with me." [9] Simon Peter said to him, "Master, then not only my feet, but my hands and head as well." [10] Jesus said to him, "Whoever has bathed has no need except to have his feet washed, for he is clean all over; so you are clean, but not all." [11] For he knew who would betray him; for this reason, he said, "Not all of you are clean."

[12] So when he had washed their feet [and] put his garments back on and reclined at table again, he said to them, "Do you realize what I have done for you? [13] You call me 'teacher' and 'master,' and rightly so, for indeed I am. [14] If I, therefore, the master and teacher, have washed your feet, you ought to wash one another's feet. [15] I have given you a model to follow, so that as I have done for you, you should also do. [16] Amen, amen, I say to you, no slave is greater than his master nor any messenger greater than the one who sent him. [17] If you understand this, blessed are you if you do it."

Comment

Washing someone's feet is a very intimate act. The disciples are fascinated and silent; some do not feel comfortable with it. Peter speaks out. When he then understands what it is all about, his resistance tips over into exuberant enthusiasm. Have a share in Jesus! Let yourself be touched by him, experience salvation through his touch!

The disciples still remember the days before the feast very well; for example, their dispute about the best places in heaven, and Jesus's admonition: "You know that those who are recognized as rulers over the Gentiles lord it over them, and their great ones make their authority over them felt. But it shall not be so among you. Rather, whoever wishes to be great among you will be your servant; whoever wishes to be first among you will be the slave of all."

After washing their feet, Jesus and the disciples have a meal. Together they celebrate the exodus of the Israelites from Egypt, from slavery to freedom. Everyone feels that this meal is not like other years; it is something very special. They are deeply impressed by Jesus's words about sharing bread and wine — words that continue to have an effect to this day. In the Last Supper Jesus creates a unique community. Bread and wine are changed and also the person who receives the changed gifts: she or he receives a share in Jesus Christ, whose life does not end with death, but is fulfilled in the resurrection. And we have a share in this transformation from death to life.

Suggestions

- First I prepare the scene for myself.
- Can I let Jesus touch me? How does Jesus touch me, how does God touch me in my life?
- In which situations do I let myself be touched?
- What does "having a share in Jesus" mean to me?
- How and when do I follow Jesus's example of service?
- What does communion mean to me?

Film

The Ninth Day – Der neunte Tag

Germany, Luxembourg 2004, 97 Min. Directed by Volker Schlöndorff

MEDITATION 4

Mark 14:32-42

[32] Then they came to a place named Gethsemane, and he said to his disciples, "Sit here while I pray." [33] He took with him Peter, James, and John, and began to be troubled and distressed. [34] Then he said to them, "My soul is sorrowful even to death. Remain here and keep watch." [35] He advanced a little and fell to the ground and prayed that if it were possible the hour might pass by him; [36] he said, "Abba, Father, all things are possible to you. Take this cup away from me, but not what I will but what you will." [37] When he returned he found them asleep. He said to Peter, "Simon, are you asleep? Could you not keep watch for one hour? [38] Watch and pray that you may not undergo the test. The spirit is willing but the flesh is weak." [39] Withdrawing again, he prayed, saying the same thing. [40] Then he returned once more and found them asleep, for they could not keep their eyes open and did not know what to answer him. [41] He returned a third time and said to them, "Are you still sleeping and taking your rest? It is enough. The hour has come. Behold, the Son of Man is to be handed over to sinners. [42] Get up, let us go. See, my betrayer is at hand."

Comment

Jesus does not want to be alone. He takes his disciples with him, and they should stand by him. But they are tired, and again and again they fall asleep. What a disappointment for Jesus!

Many theologians interpret his last hours before his arrest as teaching his obedience to the Father. But what does "be obedient" really mean here? Does God want the death of his beloved Son? Does he command Jesus to take up the cross? Is it possible to believe in such a God? Do we not always say and hear: God is love, God is relationship — Father, Son and Holy Spirit? Isn't death the end of all love, the end of every relationship?

Jesus himself gives us the key: "This is why the Father loves me, because I lay down my life in order to take it up again. No one takes it from me, but I lay it down on my own. I have power to lay it down, and power to take it up again. This command I have received from my Father."

Jesus learned obedience, by a free decision to "give his life." The Father could not take this decision away from him. He decided to wait for his captors, instead of going away — which he could have done easily, since he knew his way around Jerusalem very well. Go back to Galilee with his disciples? That would have been a trivial outcome, and the world would have forgotten Jesus of Nazareth. If he refused the "cup" of suffering, Jesus would have given in to the tempter in the end.

Suggestions

- First I prepare the scene for myself.
- Do I know lonely decisions? What consequences did they have?
- When do I feel lonely and abandoned?
- Have I been able to help other people in such situations?
- Do I sometimes escape into triviality?

Film

Jesus Christ Superstar
USA 1972, 107 Minutes. Directed by Norman Jewison

MEDITATION 5

Luke 23:26-31

[26] As they led him away they took hold of a certain Simon, a Cyrenian, who was coming in from the country; and after laying the cross on him, they made him carry it behind Jesus. [27] A large crowd of people followed Jesus, including many women who mourned and lamented him. [28] Jesus turned to them and said, "Daughters of Jerusalem, do not weep for me; weep instead for yourselves and for your children, [29] for indeed, the days are coming when people will say, 'Blessed are the barren, the wombs that never bore and the breasts that never nursed.' [30] At that time people will say to the mountains, 'Fall upon us!' and to the hills, 'Cover us!' [31] for if these things are done when the wood is green what will happen when it is dry?"

Comment

Jesus walks on his way of suffering. Weakened by the cruel scourging, he can no longer bear the cross. The soldiers force Simon of Cyrene to help Jesus. Although he only takes on the sign of shame in protest, he feels how grateful Jesus is to him for the help. The large crowd follows the "spectacle" duly screaming and bellowing, without the slightest sign of compassion.

Only few faithful women dare to show their compassion. They do not care about the rabble, nor about the Roman law, which severely punishes any signs of compassion at crucifixions. They weep and suffer with Jesus; he is not alone in his last hours. Does he also look for the disciples? Where are they, actually? They promised Jesus that they would never leave him under any circumstances. Maybe he just can't see them in the crowd.

Unexpectedly, Jesus turns to the women and warns them of future horrors that he alone foresees: the destruction of the Temple of Jerusalem, which will happen decades later — the center for worship of his beloved Father, leveled to the ground. The women must have been shocked. Even under the greatest pain and close to death, Jesus shows them that he takes part in their fate and feels with them.

Suggestions

- First I prepare the scene for myself.
- Which side of the "play" am I on? Which "role" can I take on?
- In which situations have I myself experienced suffering?
- When have I suffered with other people?
- Can I "look" at suffering, or do I rather avoid it?

Film

Of Men and Gods – Des Hommes et des Dieux
France 2010, 122 Minutes. Directed by Xavier Beauvois

MEDITATION 6

Mark 15:22-41

[22] They brought him to the place of Golgotha (which is translated Place of the Skull). [23] They gave him wine drugged with myrrh, but he did not take it. [24] Then they crucified him and divided his garments by casting lots for them to see what each should take. [25] It was nine o'clock in the morning when they crucified him. [26] The inscription of the charge against him read, "The King of the Jews." [27] With him they crucified two revolutionaries, one on his right and one on his left. [28] [29] Those passing by reviled him, shaking their heads and saying, "Aha! You who would destroy the temple and rebuild it in three days, [30] save yourself by coming down from the cross." [31] Likewise the chief priests, with the scribes, mocked him among themselves and said, "He saved others; he cannot save himself. [32] Let the Messiah, the King of Israel, come down now from the cross that we may see and believe." Those who were crucified with him also kept abusing him.

[33] At noon darkness came over the whole land until three in the afternoon. [34] And at three o'clock Jesus cried out in a loud voice, *"Eloi, Eloi, lema sabachthani?"* which is translated, "My God, my God, why have you forsaken me?" [35] Some of the bystanders who heard it said, "Look, he is calling Elijah." [36] One of them ran, soaked a sponge with wine, put it on a reed, and gave it to him to drink, saying, "Wait, let us see if Elijah comes to take him down." [37] Jesus gave a loud cry and breathed his last. [38] The veil of the sanctuary was torn in two from top to bottom. [39] When the centurion who stood facing him saw how he breathed his last he said, "Truly this man was the Son of God!" [40] There were also women looking on from a distance. Among them were Mary Magdalene, Mary the mother of the younger James and of Joses, and Salome. [41] These women had followed him when he was in Galilee and ministered to him. There were also many other women who had come up with him to Jerusalem.

Comment

The crucifixion scene has Jesus in the middle, the two criminals on his left and right. As if he had not been humiliated enough by the soldiers, he is also mocked by the chief priests, the scribes and the criminals. But Jesus prays for those who crucify him.

In the gospels we have various words of Jesus on the cross. Overwhelmed by pain, he prays with Psalm 22: "My God, my God, why have you forsaken me?" Nevertheless, he is sure that the Father will finally embrace him with his great love: "Father, into your hands I commend my spirit." Probably the last thing he says when he dies is, "It is done."

And again it is the women who do not leave Jesus even in his most difficult hour. Mary remembers the words of the aged Simeon: "But a sword will pierce your soul." Now she knows what that means.

Darkness covers the land — God's son is dead. The crowd and even the leader of the torturers, the Roman captain, is affected by the way Jesus died. It is as if he suddenly sees: "Truly, this man was the Son of God!" The drama has reached its climax. The temple curtain in front of the Holy of Holies is torn apart.

Suggestions

- First I prepare the scene for myself.
- Can I, like women, like Mary, be close to Jesus in his last hours?
- Would I rather run away? Why?
- The crowd around the cross mocks Jesus — do I know similar situations?
- Which of Jesus's last words touches me the most? Why?

Film

The Passion of the Christ
USA 2004, 127 Minutes. Directed by Mel Gibson

MEDITATION 7

John 19:38-42

[38] After this, Joseph of Arimathea, secretly a disciple of Jesus for fear of the Jews, asked Pilate if he could remove the body of Jesus. And Pilate permitted it. So he came and took his body. [39] Nicodemus, the one who had first come to him at night, also came bringing a mixture of myrrh and aloes weighing about one hundred pounds. [40] They took the body of Jesus and bound it with burial cloths along with the spices, according to the Jewish burial custom. [41] Now in the place where he had been crucified there was a garden, and in the garden a new tomb, in which no one had yet been buried. [42] So they laid Jesus there because of the Jewish preparation day; for the tomb was close by.

Comment

Joseph of Arimathea and Nicodemus take care of the body of Jesus. Painfully they carry him from Golgotha to the nearby garden. At least here they are safe from the Roman soldiers for a while.

The women who held out at the cross probably followed the two men, to offer their help. They carefully remove the crown of thorns. It has left deep traces. Then they clean and anoint the tortured body. It is the last service of love they can do for Jesus. The scent of the precious oil fills the burial cave. Then they say goodbye to their Lord and watch as the heavy stone is rolled in front of the grave. Together they go back to the room where they and the disciples celebrated the Last Supper with Jesus. At least they are not alone in their grief.

The unimaginable has happened: Jesus has been executed like a criminal. Had they not left everything behind for his sake? And now the Kingdom of God seems further away than ever. Were the three years they spent with Jesus in vain? What will happen now?

It is a very silent Sabbath that they spend together.

Suggestions

- First I prepare the scene for myself.
- Who is closest to me at the burial of Jesus?
- To pay one's last respects to a dead person meant at that time to anoint him with oil. Can I imagine doing that for Jesus? Or for someone close to me?
- Have I experienced a serious loss? How did I get over it?
- Do I remember days of mourning? What led me out of the "valley of tears" again?

Film

In Spite of Darkness. A Spiritual Encounter with Auschwitz
Germany 2008, 74 Minutes. Directed by Christof Wolf

FOURTH WEEK: RESURRECTION OF JESUS

The center of the Christian faith is the resurrection. "But if Christ has not been raised, then our preaching is empty and your faith meaningless," writes St. Paul to the Corinthians. In all four gospels there is a unanimous report: The grave is empty. Jesus then appears, first to the women. This is very astonishing, since the testimony of women at that time was not considered credible. If the authors of that time had wanted to invent something credible, they would certainly have written that Jesus showed himself first to the disciples.

When Jesus finally appears to the disciples, they do not recognize him at first. He has to reveal himself explicitly. Obviously he is changed in a way that makes recognition very difficult. The encounter with the risen Christ seems to trigger fears at first. The disciples consider Jesus to be a ghost, since he can enter through closed doors. At the same time they can touch him, and he even eats something before their eyes. But Jesus remains with them in a bodily appearance only for a short time. His Spirit, however, will fill them at Pentecost and transform the anxious disciples into courageous witnesses of faith.

The question of what awaits us after death is an age-old question of humanity. Depending on our answer, we live differently. If everything ends with death, then I must find all happiness on earth. But what if I have a long illness, or what if I die early? How do I deal with the suffering, with the defeats, with the failure in my life? What can I hope for?

God became man in Jesus Christ, and since we are the image of God, the Spirit of God lives in us. One cannot surpass God's ability to transform death into life. But it is ultimately up to our own free decision to believe in it and to use God's gift of bringing back to life what is stuck and dead.

MEDITATION 1

John 20:1-18

[1] On the first day of the week, Mary of Magdala came to the tomb early in the morning, while it was still dark, and saw the stone removed from the tomb. [2] So she ran and went to Simon Peter and to the other disciple whom Jesus loved, and told them, "They have taken the Lord from the tomb, and we don't know where they put him." [3] So Peter and the other disciple went out and came to the tomb. [4] They both ran, but the other disciple ran faster than Peter and arrived at the tomb first; [5] he bent down and saw the burial cloths there, but did not go in. [6] When Simon Peter arrived after him, he went into the tomb and saw the burial cloths there, [7] and the cloth that had covered his head, not with the burial cloths but rolled up in a separate place. [8] Then the other disciple also went in, the one who had arrived at the tomb first, and he saw and believed. [9] For they did not yet understand the scripture that he had to rise from the dead. [10] Then the disciples returned home.

[11] But Mary stayed outside the tomb weeping. And as she wept, she bent over into the tomb [12] and saw two angels in white sitting there, one at the head and one at the feet where the body of Jesus had been. [13] And they said to her, "Woman, why are you weeping?" She said to them, "They have taken my Lord, and I don't know where they laid him." [14] When she had said this, she turned around and saw Jesus there, but did not know it was Jesus. [15] Jesus said to her, "Woman, why are you weeping? Whom are you looking for?" She thought it was the gardener and said to him, "Sir, if you carried him away, tell me where you laid him, and I will take him." [16] Jesus said to her, "Mary!" She turned and said to him in Hebrew, "Rabbouni," which means Teacher. [17] Jesus said to her, "Stop holding on to me, for I have not yet ascended to the Father. But go to my brothers and tell them, 'I am going to my Father and your Father, to my God and your God.'" [18] Mary of Magdala went and announced to the disciples, "I have seen the Lord," and what he told her.

Comment

Is there even a more beautiful cry of joy than Mary's "Rabbouni," after she recognized Jesus in the supposed gardener? His voice healed her from her grief. She can hardly believe that Jesus has really risen from the dead. She would like best to embrace him, full of joy, to throw herself at the feet of the revered Master. But Jesus eludes her. His "Stop holding on to me" heralds a new relationship, one that Mary still must learn.

God's love has overcome death. Even if we die, we will be transformed like Jesus through this love. This is the promise Jesus gives us: "I am going to my Father and your Father, to my God and your God."

And Mary goes back to the other disciples and announces the good news to them. That they do not want to believe her at first is reported elsewhere. They thought it was gossip, only something people said. For shouldn't they, the men, have seen the Risen One first of all? But Jesus shows himself first to the women, to those who did not abandon him in his suffering. He remains faithful to them: "Everyone who acknowledges me before others I will acknowledge before my heavenly Father."

Suggestions

- First I prepare the scene for myself.
- Mary feels the joy of the resurrection in a very special way. Can I feel this joy and compare it with my own experiences?
- The suffering is overcome. How does the risen Jesus differ from the earthly Jesus?
- God's love overcomes death. Do I experience this love already here and now in my life?
- Do I bear witness to the risen Jesus? What situations and reactions do I remember?
- What does resurrection mean to me?

Film

Wings of Desire

Germany, France 1987, 127 Minutes. Directed by Wim Wenders

MEDITATION 2

John 20:19-29

[19] On the evening of that first day of the week, when the doors were locked, where the disciples were, for fear of the Jews, Jesus came and stood in their midst and said to them, "Peace be with you." [20] When he had said this, he showed them his hands and his side. The disciples rejoiced when they saw the Lord. [21] [Jesus] said to them again, "Peace be with you. As the Father has sent me, so I send you." [22] And when he had said this, he breathed on them and said to them, "Receive the holy Spirit. [23] Whose sins you forgive are forgiven them, and whose sins you retain are retained."

[24] Thomas, called Didymus, one of the Twelve, was not with them when Jesus came. [25] So the other disciples said to him, "We have seen the Lord." But he said to them, "Unless I see the mark of the nails in his hands and put my finger into the nailmarks and put my hand into his side, I will not believe." [26] Now a week later his disciples were again inside and Thomas was with them. Jesus came, although the doors were locked, and stood in their midst and said, "Peace be with you." [27] Then he said to Thomas, "Put your finger here and see my hands, and bring your hand and put it into my side, and do not be unbelieving, but believe." [28] Thomas answered and said to him, "My Lord and my God!" [29] Jesus said to him, "Have you come to believe because you have seen me? Blessed are those who have not seen and have believed."

Comment

Very frightened, the disciples stay together. The memory of the brutal death of Jesus on the cross is still too fresh. Perhaps they fear that the same could happen to them if they do not hide. And the fact that Mary Magdalene claims that Jesus rose from the dead and even appeared to her confuses them even more. What should they think of it? Suddenly, although all doors are closed, Jesus is standing among them and greets them in an unusual way: "Peace be with you." He shows them his stigmata so that they may recognize: Yes, it is the Lord! Clearly they can see the marks of pain.

Jesus does not send the disciples into the world to take revenge, but "as the Father has sent me, so I send you." Jesus invites forgiveness. As difficult as that may be, they will have to learn it. Even Thomas, the skeptic, has to learn something. What the others report does not sound convincing enough for him. He must see with his own eyes, and with his own hands grasp what he is supposed to believe. He has to wait for a whole week, until Jesus appears to the disciples for the second time, again using this greeting of peace, which confirms the shalom usual among the Jews in a completely new way. Thomas can hardly believe it: "My Lord and my God" is probably one of the shortest confessions of faith in the Bible. Because he sees, he believes.

"Peace be with you," says only the risen Jesus. In the liturgy we know this greeting of forgiveness, which gives an inner peace that only God can give to men.

Suggestions

- First I prepare the scene for myself.
- What does faith in the resurrection mean to me?
- Can I only believe what I see? Why?
- Do I wish I could touch Jesus like Thomas did?
- Do I know situations where my fear or impotent anger has turned into joy and forgiveness?
- When and how do I experience the inner peace of God?

Film

Adam's Apples. God Is on My Side – Adams Æbler
Denmark 2005, 95 Minutes. Directed by Anders Thomas Jensen

MEDITATION 3

Luke 24:13-35

[13] Now that very day two of them were going to a village seven miles from Jerusalem called Emmaus, [14] and they were conversing about all the things that had occurred. [15] And it happened that while they were conversing [...] Jesus himself drew near and walked with them, [16] but their eyes were prevented from recognizing him. [17] He asked them, "What are you discussing as you walk along?" They stopped, looking downcast. [18] One of them, named Cleopas, said to him in reply, "Are you the only visitor to Jerusalem who does not know of the things that have taken place there in these days?" [19] And he replied to them, "What sort of things?" They said to him, "The things that happened to Jesus the Nazarene, who was a prophet mighty in deed and word before God and all the people, [20] how our chief priests and rulers both handed him over to a sentence of death and crucified him. [21] But we were hoping that he would be the one to redeem Israel; and besides all this, it is now the third day since this took place. [22] Some women from our group, however, have astounded us: they were at the tomb early in the morning [23] and did not find his body; they came back and reported that they had indeed seen a vision of angels who announced that he was alive. [24] Then some of those with us went to the tomb and found things just as the women had described, but him they did not see." [25] And he said to them, "Oh, how foolish you are! How slow of heart to believe all that the prophets spoke! [26] Was it not necessary that the Messiah should suffer these things and enter into his glory?" [27] Then beginning with Moses and all the prophets, he interpreted to them what referred to him in all the scriptures. [28] As they approached the village to which they were going, he gave the impression that he was going on farther. [29] But they urged him, "Stay with us, for it is nearly evening and the day is almost over." So he went in to stay with them. [30] And it happened that, while he was with them at table, he took bread, said the blessing, broke it, and gave it to them. [31] With that their eyes were opened and they recognized him, but he vanished from their sight. [32] Then they said to each other, "Were not our hearts burning [within us] while he spoke to us on the way and opened the scriptures to us?" [33] So they set out at once and returned to Jerusalem where they found gathered together the eleven and those with them [34] who were saying, "The Lord has truly been raised and has appeared to Simon!" [35] Then the two recounted what had taken place on the way and how he was made known to them in the breaking of the bread.

Comment

Although the two disciples heard what the women reported, they cannot believe that Jesus has risen from the dead. They have been so disappointed in their expectations of salvation that they are blind to another reality. Tired and beaten they go home. On the way Jesus joins them. In doing so, he fulfilled what he had promised at the Last Supper in his intercession for the disciples: "When I was with them I protected them in your name that you gave me, and I guarded them, and none of them was lost except the son of destruction, in order that the scripture might be fulfilled."

Now he makes it come true. No one should be lost, not even these two, who are in danger of sinking into their pain. They do not recognize Jesus, but they are so fascinated by him and his speech that they can not simply let him go, but want to show him their hospitality. And there it happens: When Jesus breaks the bread and speaks the divine praise, the familiar gesture suddenly makes clear to them what their hearts have suspected all along. In the moment of thanksgiving they recognize Jesus. The fact that he immediately withdraws from their gazes cannot cloud their joy. They set off immediately and hurry back to Jerusalem to join the others. So the women were right after all! And they are glad to find the others all together to hear the report: The Lord has also appeared to us.

Suggestions

- First I prepare the scene for myself.
- Jesus takes care of the disappointed disciples. Do I know situations where Jesus was looking for me?
- Jesus is with the disciples on their way. Does Jesus accompany me in my everyday life? How do I recognize this?
- For where two or three are gathered together in my name, there am I in the midst of them, says Jesus. What does fellowship in faith mean to me?
- What goes on in me when I celebrate Eucharist (which means "thanksgiving")? Do I perhaps, like the disciples, suddenly recognize connections that I was not aware of before?

Film

One Step at a Time: On Foot to Jerusalem
Germany 2012, 52 Minutes. Directed by Christof Wolf

MEDITATION 4

Luke 24:36-49

[36] While they were still speaking about this, he stood in their midst and said to them, "Peace be with you." [37] But they were startled and terrified and thought that they were seeing a ghost. [38] Then he said to them, "Why are you troubled? And why do questions arise in your hearts? [39] Look at my hands and my feet, that it is I myself. Touch me and see, because a ghost does not have flesh and bones as you can see I have." [40] And as he said this, he showed them his hands and his feet. [41] While they were still incredulous for joy and were amazed, he asked them, "Have you anything here to eat?" [42] They gave him a piece of baked fish; [43] he took it and ate it in front of them. [44] He said to them, "These are my words that I spoke to you while I was still with you, that everything written about me in the law of Moses and in the prophets and psalms must be fulfilled." [45] Then he opened their minds to understand the scriptures. [46] And he said to them, "Thus it is written that the Messiah would suffer and rise from the dead on the third day [47] and that repentance, for the forgiveness of sins, would be preached in his name to all the nations, beginning from Jerusalem. [48] You are witnesses of these things. [49] And [behold] I am sending the promise of my Father upon you; but stay in the city until you are clothed with power from on high."

Comment

The disciples still doubt — so much that they think Jesus is a ghost when he comes to them in the flesh. It is very similar to the time when he met them on the Sea of Galilee over the water. Now the Risen One must show them his pierced hands and feet so that they may recognize in him the crucified one. Jesus also eats before their eyes — a spirit would not be able to do this. And yet they know the Scriptures, in which all these things were foretold.

But Jesus wants them to participate in the transforming power of the resurrection. His central message is the forgiveness of sins. Whoever can accept it, and forgive the other, makes a new beginning possible. In this way Jesus gives inner peace, making everything new.

Jesus feels the fear of his disciples. They cannot and need not do this on their own. They are to remain in Jerusalem, where support from his Father, the Holy Spirit, will come upon them. At Pentecost this promise will be fulfilled. The fearful disciples are then transformed into powerful proclaimers of the joyful message of Jesus.

Suggestions

- First I prepare the scene for myself.
- Would I touch the wounds of Jesus if I could?
- Do I experience the grace of forgiveness of sins in my life? Do I give forgiveness?
- Have I ever been able to start over because someone has forgiven me?
- The Holy Spirit filled the disciples at Pentecost. When do I feel the Spirit of God in me and when not?

Film

Flatliners
USA 1990, 110 Minutes. Directed by Joel Schumacher

MEDITATION 5

John 21:1-14

[1] After this, Jesus revealed himself again to his disciples at the Sea of Tiberias. He revealed himself in this way. [2] Together were Simon Peter, Thomas called Didymus, Nathanael from Cana in Galilee, Zebedee's sons, and two others of his disciples. [3] Simon Peter said to them, "I am going fishing." They said to him, "We also will come with you." So they went out and got into the boat, but that night they caught nothing. [4] When it was already dawn, Jesus was standing on the shore; but the disciples did not realize that it was Jesus. [5] Jesus said to them, "Children, have you caught anything to eat?" They answered him, "No." [6] So he said to them, "Cast the net over the right side of the boat and you will find something." So they cast it, and were not able to pull it in because of the number of fish. [7] So the disciple whom Jesus loved said to Peter, "It is the Lord." When Simon Peter heard that it was the Lord, he tucked in his garment, for he was lightly clad, and jumped into the sea. [8] The other disciples came in the boat, for they were not far from shore, only about a hundred yards, dragging the net with the fish. [9] When they climbed out on shore, they saw a charcoal fire with fish on it and bread. [10] Jesus said to them, "Bring some of the fish you just caught." [11] So Simon Peter went over and dragged the net ashore full of one hundred fifty-three large fish. Even though there were so many, the net was not torn. [12] Jesus said to them, "Come, have breakfast." And none of the disciples dared to ask him, "Who are you?" because they realized it was the Lord. [13] Jesus came over and took the bread and gave it to them, and in like manner the fish. [14] This was now the third time Jesus was revealed to his disciples after being raised from the dead.

Comment

At the lake of Tiberias the circle closes. It is the home of the disciples, where Jesus called Simon Peter and the other disciples to follow him. Now he is here to fulfill his promise to make them fishers of men. And again they do not recognize Jesus at first. Only when they, at his word, throw out their nets and make a huge catch (as they did at their first meeting), do the eyes of John's favorite disciple open. He recognizes the Lord.

The unbelievable fishing catch lets the disciples experience in everyday life that even seemingly hopeless situations can change if they listen to Jesus. "Behold, I make all things new," says the Revelation of John. The new heaven and the new earth became reality with Jesus's resurrection. Death does not have the last word.

Suggestions

- First I prepare the scene for myself.
- If I went for a walk with Jesus at the lake of Tiberias, how might our conversation go? Do I have a question that I would like to ask Jesus?
- Jesus comes in the middle of the everyday life of the disciples, and at first they do not recognize him. Am I also sometimes blind to God's presence in my everyday life? What prevents me from meeting God, Jesus?
- Has it ever happened to me that I was only successful at the moment when I no longer believed in success and gave up? Why has something changed?
- Relationships are something dynamic, and there is always the potential for change in them. How alive are my relationships? Do I want change? Why?

Film

Babette's Feast – Babettes Gaestebud
Denmark 1987, 99 Minutes. Directed by Gabriel Axel

MEDITATION 6

John 21:15-19

[15] When they had finished breakfast, Jesus said to Simon Peter, "Simon, son of John, do you love me more than these?" He said to him, "Yes, Lord, you know that I love you." He said to him, "Feed my lambs." [16] He then said to him a second time, "Simon, son of John, do you love me?" He said to him, "Yes, Lord, you know that I love you." He said to him, "Tend my sheep." [17] He said to him the third time, "Simon, son of John, do you love me?" Peter was distressed that he had said to him a third time, "Do you love me?" and he said to him, "Lord, you know everything; you know that I love you." [Jesus] said to him, "Feed my sheep. [18] Amen, amen, I say to you, when you were younger, you used to dress yourself and go where you wanted; but when you grow old, you will stretch out your hands, and someone else will dress you and lead you where you do not want to go." [19] He said this signifying by what kind of death he would glorify God. And when he had said this, he said to him, "Follow me."

Comment

When Jesus asks Peter the question three times, you still hear the crowing of the cock in your ear. This is Peter, who leaves everything behind for Jesus and follows Jesus unconditionally, the man of little faith who is afraid of his own courage and sinks into the water, who confesses Jesus as Messiah, who tempts Jesus and is rejected by Jesus as Satan, who at first does not want to have his feet washed, who falls asleep with the other disciples in Gethsemane, who fights with the sword for Jesus and in his overzealousness cuts off an ear of the servant of the high priest, who denies Jesus three times and whom Jesus calls the rock on which he wants to build his church. One can well imagine how much this Peter is shamed by hearing the same question three times. He wants so much to make amends and give back nothing but love. Will he be up to the pastoral ministry that Jesus entrusts to him?

Suggestions

- First I prepare the scene for myself.
- If Jesus asked this question to me in the same way on repeated occasions, how would I answer?
- When was the last time I myself said "I love you"? To whom?
- What can I give back to Jesus?
- When I look back on my life, do I remember above all some happy moments, or dark times?
- Have I once failed because I lost my courage? What has given me confidence again?
- Jesus does not prophesy a happy ending for Peter. How do I imagine the end of my life?

Film

The Straight Story
USA 1999, 111 Minutes. Directed by David Lynch

MEDITATION 7

Prayer for the Attainment of Love

Take, Lord, and receive all my liberty, my memory, my understanding, and my entire will. All I have and call my own, you have given to me. To you, Lord, I return it. Everything is yours; do with it what you will. Give me only your love and your grace, that is enough for me.

Ignatius of Loyola

Comment

A teacher of the Law asks Jesus about the most important commandment in the Law. Jesus answers him with two quotations from the Old Testament: "The first is: Hear Israel, the LORD our God, the LORD alone! Therefore, you shall love the LORD, your God, with all your heart, with all your soul, with all your mind and with all your strength" (Dt 6:4-5). The second is: "You shall love your neighbor as yourself. No other commandment is greater than these two" (Lev 19:18). This double commandment of love ultimately summarizes the Ten Commandments and also shows the dynamics that are inherent in the relationship with God. Just as we love God, we should also love ourselves and our fellow human beings. It is in love that our image of God is most clearly visible. The love of God radiates from a person who loves.

Prayer for the attainment of love is the heart of the final exercise of the fourth week, the contemplation for the attainment of love. Important are the two preliminary remarks of Ignatius: "Love must be put more into works than into words." If it remains only lip service, what use are the beautiful flowery words and promises? The second: "Love consists in communication from both sides: namely, that the lover gives and communicates to the beloved what he has, or of what he has or can; just as vice versa the beloved gives to the lover."

Now the praying person is invited to imagine the beauty of creation, the gift of God to mankind; the redemption through Jesus Christ; or his own life with its talents and abilities given by God. When I look at my own life, I discover not only God's faithfulness to me, but also that God wants to continue giving himself to me. God answers me; God wants to meet me at eye level. My love for God is not a one-way street; it goes both ways. Certain of this, I can surrender to God with all my heart. Everything in my life is given to me by God; everything I put back into his hands. I can also entrust my pain and suffering to God. Only his love and his grace can give me the peace that the world cannot give. If I can pray in this way, then my devotion is transformed into what is probably the greatest inner freedom. Love overcomes all fear and sadness, it lets me shape my world. God's love, justice, goodness, kindness and mercy shows itself in me and thus in this world.

Suggestions

- First I prepare the scene for myself.
- St. Paul's Hymn to Love says: "Love is patient, love is kind. [...] It bears all things, believes all things, hopes all things, endures all things. Love never fails." Am I experiencing this in my life, in my relationships, in my relationship with God?
- Can I entrust and leave everything to God? What prevents me from doing so?
- What has God given me in my life? What do I give to God?

Film

Three Colors: Red – Trois Couleurs: Rouge
France, Switzerland, Poland 1994, 99 Minutes.
Directed by Krzysztof Kieślowski

EPILOGUE

by Josef Schmidt, S.J.

The silence of the retreat leads us into the desert. Everything else that surrounds and occupies us is suddenly no longer there — only emptiness. Only God! In this desert Jesus experiences his oneness with God. And we, by following him there, discover with him: God alone is enough! This is the first commandment, the experience of Moses at Sinai. In the experience of this exclusiveness we understand our own uniqueness. We comprehend our freedom, we understand ourselves to be from God, if we align ourselves completely with him. Then that independence is given to us, which Ignatius calls "indifference."

God does not give up on us. He trusts us to take our life into our own hands in order to reshape it by a good and free choice. And yet — how is the good choice to be made? It is a matter of listening to the One who has given us into our own hands, so that we can feel ourselves as the gift that we are and that we can only grasp and keep if we are willing to pass it on to others. By sharing God's generosity, we gain the freedom to give, just as he gave himself to us as a human being. What form this giving will take in our personal lives we may learn in the call of the divine giver. We then choose because we have been chosen by him, who has chosen us first.

We remember the events of life, and look with our heart at how He showed Himself to people, how He dealt with them, how He helped them, healed them, suffered with them, rejoiced with them and celebrated with them. This is how God acts with us and for us. He includes our freedom in this action, because his call to us must be answered with a free yes. It goes without saying that it cannot be a matter of simply copying the action of Jesus onto us. His invitation to follow him opens us to a way of life that is right for us personally and also in accordance with being his disciple.

The retreat leads into the "contemplation for the attainment of love." It is the great thanksgiving for the way we were allowed to go, trusting that the hand that guided us will continue to accompany us in our daily lives. We grasp life as "given" in the literal sense, as a gift of our Creator, in which He gives Himself. Let us listen once again to the text from the book of Exercises (No. 235): We "consider how God dwells in creatures: in the elements, by giving them existence; in the plants, by giving them life; in animals, by giving them sensual perception; in humans, by giving them spiritual insight."

The orientation toward God, to which we were called in the beginning of the Exercises, has made us recognize a God who turns to us and who gives himself to all of us and to me personally: "And so also to me: as he gives me existence, animates me, awakens my senses and gives me spiritual insight, as he likewise makes a temple of me, since I was created in the image and likeness of his divine majesty." We are therefore the house that God builds for us, and which he himself wants to inhabit. We are his "temple," as Ignatius says in allusion to a Pauline expression (1 Cor 3:16). How awe-inspiring should we appear to ourselves and to each other, treating each other accordingly! "Temple" is also an aesthetic term. Couldn't our spirit realize how divinely beautiful man is and how glorious our fellow man is? How could this have been revealed to us from anywhere else than from the light of that faith whose rays have fallen on us in these weeks?

ACKNOWLEDGMENTS

All bible passages and suggestions for prayer are based on my own experience. They are a selection from my "Long Retreat" in Los Angeles in 2009.

This time was a spiritual new beginning for me. Since then I have been intensively engaged in the philosophy of Alfred North Whitehead (1861-1947), the founder of process philosophy. In "Process and Reality. An Essay in Cosmology" he creates one of the most fascinating metaphysical designs proposed in our time. Building on Whitehead's philosophy, process theology has developed a new direction in theology. Two books in particular have become very important to me: "Process Theology. An Introductory Exposition" by theologian John B. Cobb and philosopher David Ray Griffin, and "Transforming Process Theism" by Lewis S. Ford.

These experiences would not have been possible for me without my Jesuit companions Mark Ravizza, S.J. and John D. Murphy, S.J. I would also like to thank Godehard Brüntrup, S.J., who is more to me than I can express here; Monika Gatt, whose fine watercolors make this book more visual; my editor Claudia Auffenberg and the Bonifatius-Verlag for the great support and the trust they have placed in me; Margret Mellert for her patient proofreading; and Daniel Jamros, S.J. for his congenial translation.

SOURCES AND BIBLIOGRAPHY

Cobb, John B., and David R. Griffin. *Process Theology. An Introductory Exposition*. Westminster Press, 1976.

Feld, Helmut. *Ignatius von Loyola: Gründer des Jesuitenordens*. Köln, Weimar, Wien und Böhlau 2006.

Ford, Lewis S. *Transforming Process Theism*. State University of New York Press, 2000.

Ignatius of Loyola. *Exerzitienbuch des Ignatius von Loyola: Geistliche Übungen*. Übersetzt von Peter Knauer. Würzburg 1998.

Ignatius von Loyola. Mystiker, Ordensgründer, Reformator. Ein Hörbild von Walter Rupp SJ. Steyl Medien / Echter Verlag 2006.

Kierkegaard, Sören. *Entweder – Oder. Ein Lebensfragment*. Herausgegeben von Victor Eremita. dtv, München 1975.

Kleist, Heinrich von. „Über die allmähliche Verfertigung der Gedanken beim Reden." In *Heinrich von Kleist. Werke in einem Band*. Carl Hanser Verlag München, 6. Auflage 1996.

New American Bible, Revised Edition © 2010, 1991, 1986, 1970 Confraternity of Christian Doctrine, Washington, D.C.

Pessoa, Fernando. *Buch der Unruhe des Hilfsbuchhalters Fernando Soares*. Hrsg. von Richard Zenith. Aus dem Portugiesischen übersetzt und revidiert von Inés Koebel, Zürich 2010.

Platon. *Sämtliche Werke*. Hrsg. von E. Grassi, Band 1, *Apologie*. Rowohlt, Hamburg 1957.

Satir, Virginia. *Making Contact*. © Celestial Arts, Berkely, California 1976.

Whitehead, Alfred North. *Process and Reality. An Essay in Cosmology*. Corrected, second edition by Donald W. Sherburne and David R. Griffin. The Free Press, New York, 1929/1978.

Film-Retreats (German): www.film-exerzitien.org

LIST OF WATERCOLORS

Cover page: Light Study in Venice III (Lichtstudie in Venedig III), Monika Gatt, watercolor red blue, 79 x 58 cm, 2013

Black and white pictures, details: Montagne SainteVictoire, Monika Gatt, watercolor, 125 x 145 cm, 2021

The watercolors by Monika Gatt can be found fully at:
www.grosse-exerzitien.org

IGNATIUS - the Godseeker

A Film by Christof Wolf, S.J.

Perhaps you have known the Jesuits for some time and you have even been helped by a Jesuits on a personal level? Many have asked what the "secret" (of the Jesuits) might be. The "secret" is a profound way of seeking God: the Spiritual Exercises. They were developed by a former soldier and eventual saint, Ignatius of Loyola, the founder of the Jesuits.

At the pinnacle of his military career, Ignatius of Loyola was thrown off course by a serious injury. He began to ponder the meaning of life, questioning his former priorities. He discovered that following Christ meant more to him than fame and wealth. After he recovered from his injury of 1521, Ignatius spent one year in Manresa (Spain). He devoted his time to seeking God and to finding out what God had in store for his future.

In the following summer, meditating in a cave at the Cardoner River, he had a deep mystical experience which changed his life forever. Now he knew what God wanted him to do. Soon after this, he began assembling young men who were in search of a more authentic Christian life. Out of this initial group, the Jesuits (the Society of Jesus) were eventually formed. Later, his fellow Jesuits said that Saint Ignatius experienced and wrote down the core of his Spiritual Exercises while in Manresa. Up to this day, the Ignatian Exercises are the spiritual foundation for all Jesuits world-wide. They have also inspired thousands of people who have been touched by Jesuit spirituality in so many ways.

In 2022 we celebrate the 500th anniversary of this profound spiritual event in Manresa, which eventually changed the Catholic Church and the world.

Ignatius – the God Seeker – discovers in his mystical experience at the river Cardoner that God is not to be found merely in scripture or tradition, but God is truly present in everything. (As the British Jesuit and poet, Gerard Manley Hopkins (1844-1889), once wrote: "The world is charged with the grandeur of God." Thus, God is not to be found in negating the world, but by discovering, embracing, and loving the world. This is the powerful message of the Jesuits, a message that up to this today can change the Catholic Church by making it more mystical, more open, more embracing, and above all more loving.

The film visualizes the essential insights and dynamics of an Ignatian retreat. In particular it takes up the image-world of Ignatius in three particularly typical exercises: "Contemplation on the Incarnation", "Meditation on Two Standards," and "Contemplation for the Attainment of Love". These three image-worlds are animated as large paintings. They are followed by short stories which translate the basic dynamics of the Exercises into the present: What does it mean that God became man (Incarnation)? What is heaven or hell for a modern day audience? Which leading figures do we follow today, who is the devil or savior for us? Finally, where do we experience God's love and his great creation?

<h1 align="center">More information online:
www.ignatius-godseeker.org</h1>

Cautela!*

Strengthen Prevention - Promote Healing

It is with great pleasure that we have taken notice of your great commitment to the protection of children and young people from sexual violence. The prevention project "Cautela! Strengthening Prevention - Promoting Healing" includes material that has obviously been prepared with a great deal of effort and professional care. For this we congratulate you quite distinctly.

Johannes Rörig

The Independent Commissioner for Child Sexual Abuse Issues

*comes from lat. cautelare and means: "Protect!" - Illustration: Felicitas Richter

Cautela! Strengthen Prevention - Promote Healing is a multidimensional learning program that aims to raise awareness of issues such as abuse and bullying and thus help protect the dignity and integrity of young people. To reach children and adults on an emotional level, it uses the specific possibilities of films. This is more successful than a purely text-based learning approach. The program consists of three films — one each for children, for teachers and for parents — and a workbook. It is aimed primarily at teachers, since schools are the biggest interface with children and parents. Of course, *Cautela!* can also be used outside schools, for example in dioceses or other institutions that want to carry out prevention work.

The *Cautela!* project was developed in cooperation with the Pater-Rupert-Mayer-Gymnasium in Pullach (Germany), and the films as well as the workbook have been tested in practice.

    Film for Teachers (10'48")
    Film for Students (4th-7th grade, 8'28")
    Film for Parents (8'20")

All films and workbooks are available (German) online at:

www.cautela.info

GOD SEEKER (APP & WEBSITE)

WHAT HOLDS THE WORLD TOGETHER AT ITS CORE

There are 7 billion people on our planet. Most of them believe in God or a higher being. But nobody has ever seen God. Is the belief in God only an illusion? Is it even worth looking for God? When the first Russian astronaut circled the Earth in his spaceship, he sparked down: "There is no God, there is no one up here!" But that seems like the wrong place to look. Nobody believes that God is floating around in space like an alien. Then where is He? Is it even reasonable to believe in something you can't see, hear or taste? For many people, however, religion is of great importance in their lives. Therefore, the question of whether it is reasonable to search for God is not just a superfluous, unworldly brooding. It is an exciting question that concerns us all.

The *God Seeker* does not make any preliminary decisions, it invites us to make our own discoveries and reflections. It is divided into four areas: God, Soul, World and World-View. If you click on a segment, further segments (questions) open up. You can "unscrew" them on a wheel. By double-clicking on a question you get a short introductory text, videos of individual philosophers and other philosophical positions appropriate to the question.

You can also test your philosophical knowledge. Check your philosophical positions by means of the quiz! Which philosophers do you agree with the most? Are you more the Plato type, or do you think more like Kant, or even maybe like Wittgenstein? You might also discover a thinker you didn't know, such as Edith Stein or Alfred N. Whitehead. Expand your philosophical horizon. Whatever you decide in the end, the *God Seeker* will help you to give good reasons for your choice.

The *God Seeker* is primarily intended for tablets, but works also on larger smartphones. Available in the Apple App Store and Google Play Store or on the Internet: *www.analytic-theology.org*

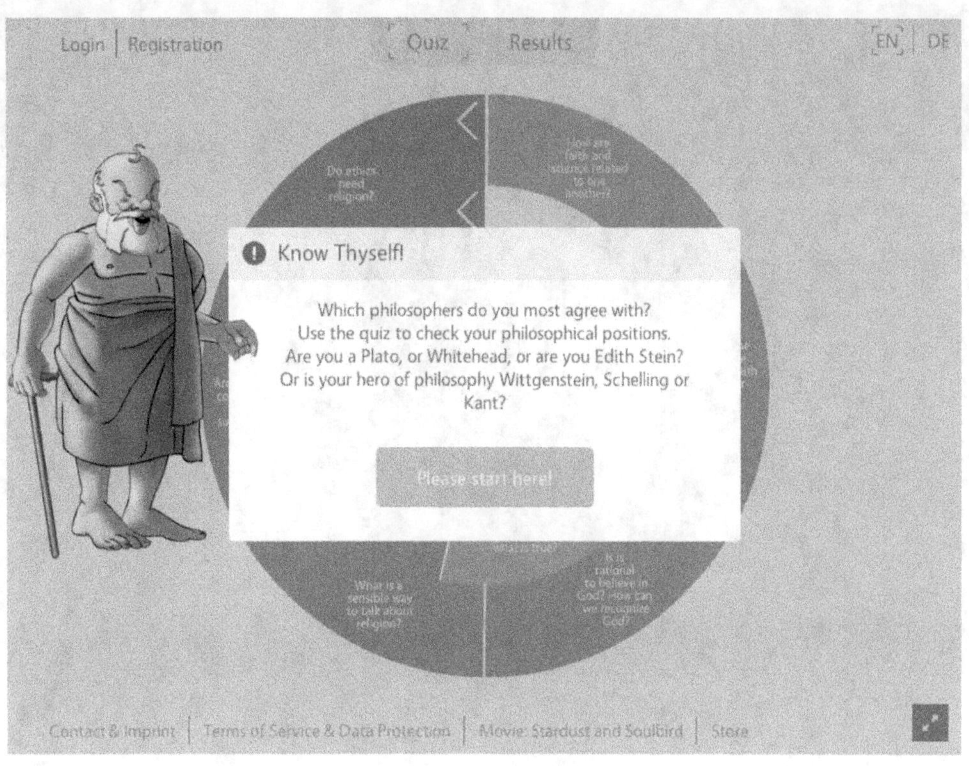

Login | Registration
Quiz
Results
EN | DE
Do ethics need religion?
How are faith and science related to one another?
Know Thyself!
Which philosophers do you most agree with?
Use the quiz to check your philosophical positions.
Are you a Plato, or Whitehead, or are you Edith Stein?
Or is your hero of philosophy Wittgenstein, Schelling or Kant?
Please start here!
What is a sensible way to talk about religion?
Is it rational to believe in God? How can we recognize God?
Contact & Imprint | Terms of Service & Data Protection | Movie: Stardust and Soulbird | Store

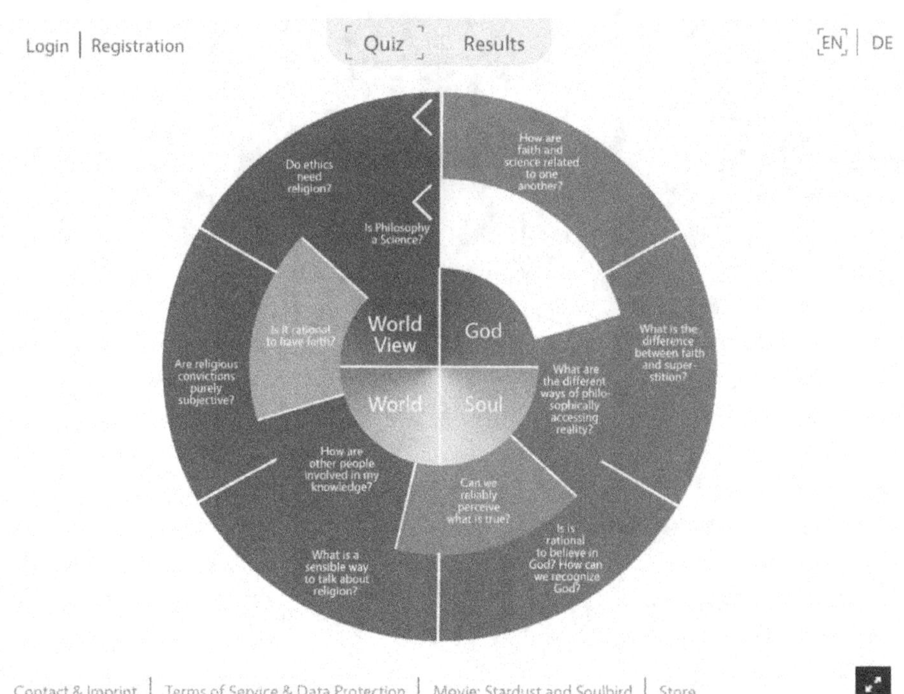

Login | Registration
Quiz
Results
EN | DE
Do ethics need religion?
How are faith and science related to one another?
Is Philosophy a Science?
Is it rational to have faith?
World View
God
Are religious convictions purely subjective?
What is the difference between faith and super-stition?
World
Soul
What are the different ways of philo-sophically accessing reality?
How are other people involved in my knowledge?
Can we reliably perceive what is true?
What is a sensible way to talk about religion?
Is is rational to believe in God? How can we recognize God?
Contact & Imprint | Terms of Service & Data Protection | Movie: Stardust and Soulbird | Store

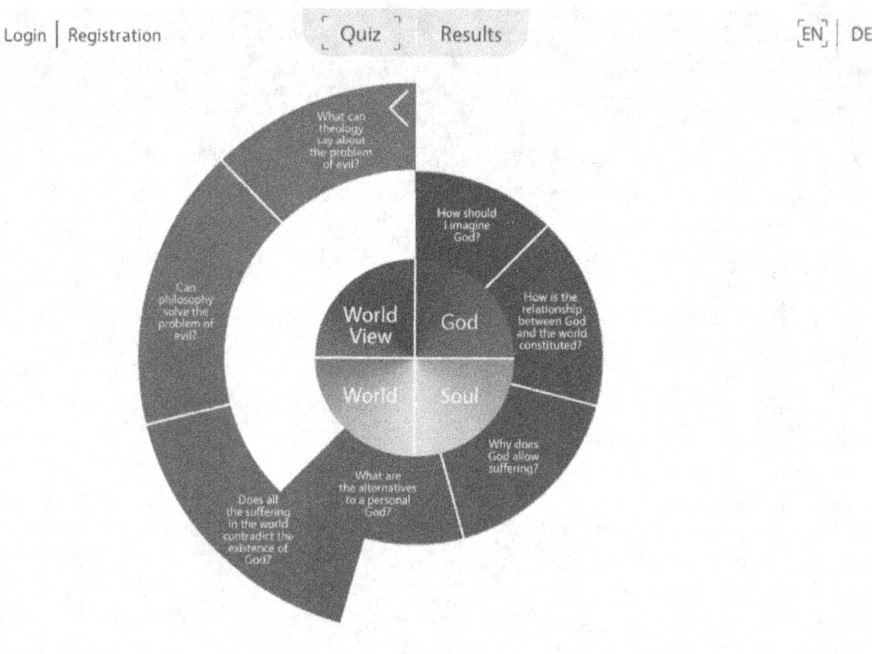

Contact & Imprint | Terms of Service & Data Protection | Movie: Stardust and Soulbird | Store

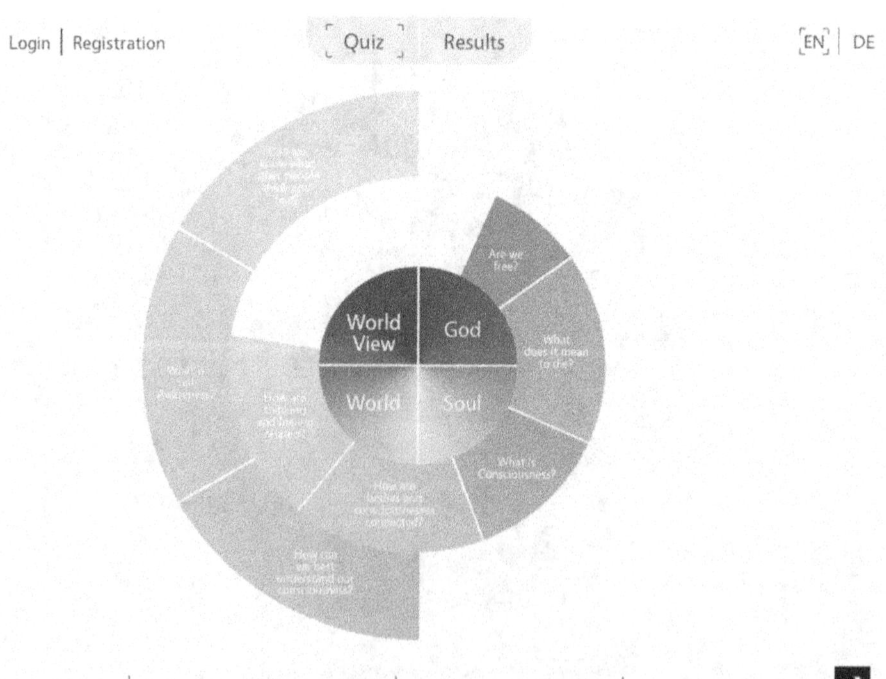

Contact & Imprint | Terms of Service & Data Protection | Movie: Stardust and Soulbird | Store

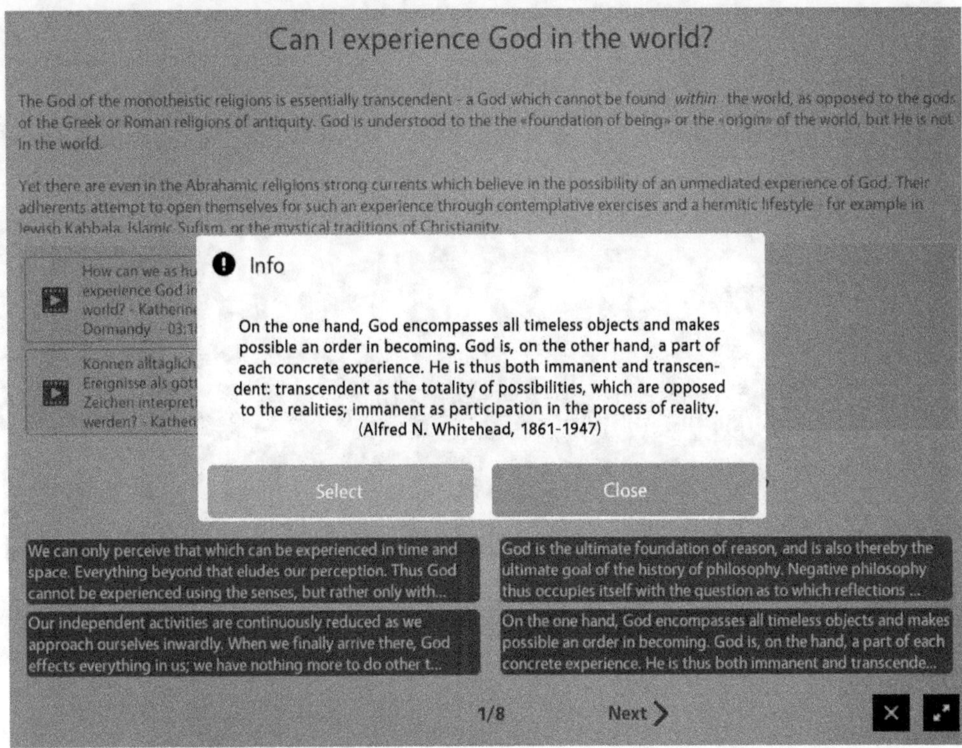
Can I experience God in the world?

The God of the monotheistic religions is essentially transcendent - a God which cannot be found within the world, as opposed to the gods of the Greek or Roman religions of antiquity. God is understood to the the «foundation of being» or the «origin» of the world, but He is not in the world.

Yet there are even in the Abrahamic religions strong currents which believe in the possibility of an unmediated experience of God. Their adherents attempt to open themselves for such an experience through contemplative exercises and a hermitic lifestyle - for example in Jewish Kabbala, Islamic Sufism, or the mystical traditions of Christianity.

How can we as hu
experience God in
world? - Katherine
Dormandy   03:1

Können alltäglich
Ereignisse als gött
Zeichen interpreti
werden? - Kathed

Info

On the one hand, God encompasses all timeless objects and makes possible an order in becoming. God is, on the other hand, a part of each concrete experience. He is thus both immanent and transcendent: transcendent as the totality of possibilities, which are opposed to the realities; immanent as participation in the process of reality.
(Alfred N. Whitehead, 1861-1947)

Select

Close

We can only perceive that which can be experienced in time and space. Everything beyond that eludes our perception. Thus God cannot be experienced using the senses, but rather only with...

God is the ultimate foundation of reason, and is also thereby the ultimate goal of the history of philosophy. Negative philosophy thus occupies itself with the question as to which reflections ...

Our independent activities are continuously reduced as we approach ourselves inwardly. When we finally arrive there, God effects everything in us; we have nothing more to do other t...

On the one hand, God encompasses all timeless objects and makes possible an order in becoming. God is, on the hand, a part of each concrete experience. He is thus both immanent and transcende...

1/8   Next >

< Back
Audio on >

Alfred N. Whitehead
1861 - 1947

My Result: 33,33%

CALLIOPE

14.29%
14.29%
19.05%
14.29%
9.52%
4.76%
9.52%
14.29%

16.67%
0%
0%
0%
16.67%
16.67%
16.67%

Save Results >

Stardust and Soulbird

An Award Winning Modern Philosophical Road Movie

Linda (yoga teacher) and her friend Andy (investment banker) are looking forward to their holidays together. But Linda's grandmother dies unexpectedly. Linda now wants to fulfill her grandmother's last will and testament. Their holidays are far away... The animated film "Stardust and Soulbird" is a philosophical road movie. The film deals with questions such as: How can we experience God in the world? Does it make sense to want to explain everything scientifically? Is the death of a loved one a proof against the existence of God?

The animated film was awarded a bronze Telly Award in 2020 as particularly inspiring.

www.sternenstaub-seelenvogel.de